Authentic Alaska

AMERICAN INDIAN LIVES

Authentic Alaska

Voices of
Its Native Writers

Susan B. Andrews & John Creed

University of Nebraska Press : Lincoln & London

⊗ The paper in this book meets the
minimum requirements of American National Standard for Information Sciences – Permanence of
Paper for Printed Library Materials,
ANSI z39.48-1984

Library of Congress Cataloging-
in-Publication Data
Authentic Alaska : voices of its
native writers / [edited by] Susan
B. Andrews and John Creed.
p. cm. — (American Indian lives)
Includes index.
ISBN 0-8032-1041-8 (cloth : alk.
paper) — ISBN 0-8032-5933-6
(pbk : alk. paper)
1. Eskimos — Alaska — Social life
and customs. 2. Eskimos —
Alaska — Biography. 3. Athapascan Indians — Alaska — Social
life and customs. 4. Athapascan
Indians — Alaska — Biography.
5. Alaska — Social conditions.
I. Andrews, Susan B., 1959- .
II. Creed, John, 1952- . III. Series.
E99.E7A87 1998 979.8′004971 —
dc21 97-21791 CIP

SECOND PRINTING 1998

Few will have the greatness to bend history itself; but each of us can work to change a small portion of events, and in the total of all those acts will be written the history of this generation. — ROBERT F. KENNEDY, 1925–1968

Contents

Photographs

Acknowledgments

University of Alaska, Staff of Chukchi College, Kotzebue, Alaska: Susan Gal, Sandra Russell, Byrd Norton, May Kenworthy, Molly Sheldon; Stacey Glaser, Library Director; Lynn Johnson, Director

Chukchi College Community Advisory Council: Barbara Armstrong, Margaret Frazier, Paula Mills, Margaret Hanson, Pete Schaeffer, Delores "Dude" Lincoln

Alaska Native Language Center, UAF: Professor Michael Krauss; Helen Howard, Administrative Assistant

Staff of Alaska and Polar Regions Archives, Elmer E. Rasmuson Library, UAF; Professor John Whitehead, History Department, UAF

Ralph Gabrielli, Executive Dean, College of Rural Alaska, UAF; Joan Wadlow, Chancellor, University of Alaska Fairbanks; Jerome Komisar, President, University of Alaska Statewide System; Stacy and Karl Puckett, formerly of the Arctic Sounder, Kotzebue, Alaska; Larry Campbell, University of Alaska Anchorage; A. J. McClanahan, formerly of the Tundra Times, Anchorage, Alaska; Len Anderson, formerly of KOTZ-AM radio, Kotzebue, Alaska; Jim Paulin, formerly of the Arctic Sounder, Kotzebue, Alaska; Cindy Nafpliotus, formerly of the University of Alaska Fairbanks Sun-Star; Don Hunter and David Hulen, Anchorage Daily News

Helen D. Reavis and Dalton K. Fine, Scarola and Reavis, New York; Julie Metz, Julie Metz Design, New York; Lynn Quitman Troyka, New York; Richard Holeton, Stanford University; Reese Cleghorn, University of Maryland, President, American Journalism Review

Mrs. Ethel Kennedy and the late Robert F. Kennedy; Erin Scully, Robert F. Kennedy Memorial, Washington DC; Kathleen Kennedy Townsend, Lieutenant Governor, State of Maryland

Ruthie Sampson, Northwest Arctic Borough School District, Kotzebue, Alaska; MayAnn Williams, Chukchi Honors Program, Kotzebue, Alaska

xiv
Acknowledgments

Pete and Polly Schaeffer, Kotzebue, Alaska consistency

The University of Alaska President's Special Projects Fund, and the University of Alaska Foundation, for support of the photographic work

Chukchi Campus, College of Rural Alaska, UAF, for support of the project and students

Sherman and Nina Carter, formerly of the University of Alaska Fairbanks, for their generous support of this project

The late Myles Horton of Highlander Folk School in Newmarket, Tennessee, and the late Howard Rock, founder and editor of the *Tundra Times*, for their inspiration

Jim Magdanz, photographer, Nome, Alaska; Steve Werle, photography assistant, Noatak, Alaska

All student participants in Chukchi News and Information Service, since the publication project's inception in 1988 at Chukchi College, Kotzebue, Alaska

Special thanks to our Elders, families, and children

Introduction

On a gravel spit a mile or so long and a half-mile wide in the extreme northwestern corner of the North American continent, an ancient Iñupiaq (Eskimo) settlement called Kikiktagruk has for centuries sat precariously on Alaska's arctic coastline, remote even by Alaska standards.

Kikiktagruk, which means "almost an island" in Iñupiaq, is today called Kotzebue, after a nineteenth-century arctic explorer, Otto von Kotzebue, who is part of a long line of outsider contact that has changed the Iñupiat forever.[1] Kotzebue, surrounded by pristine mountain and tundra wilderness, is also buffeted to the west by the frigid and treacherous Chukchi Sea that separates Alaska from Russia.

Since prehistoric times, the nomadic Iñupiat have gathered on this treeless spit during the brief, ice-free summer months to fish and hunt, to trade, and to escape the merciless mosquitoes upriver. Indeed, some families still migrate each summer from upriver villages to their coastal camps in and around Kotzebue. On this wind-battered little finger of land that juts into Kotzebue Sound some 30 miles inside the Arctic Circle and 175 miles from Russia's easternmost tip, a hardy indigenous population has sustained life successfully across the centuries in this seemingly unforgiving northern land where few others could have survived so well for so long.

This anthology of Alaska Native writers attests to a continuation of that spirit of survival, as shared by Native peoples from all across Alaska, despite the turmoil of cultural upheaval brought on for more than a century by Euro-American civilization.[2] At the dawn of the twenty-first century, the writers in this anthology capture a way of life that finds them, along with many but not all of their contemporaries, retaining strong ties to their traditional Native cultures while negotiating their way in the dominant Western world.

In particular, these writers bear witness to a significant change among their people in the latter part of the twentieth century. In rural Alaska, Natives have had to adapt to the demands of a cash economy brought on by each successive wave of economic activity, and which have been especially escalated by the 1968 discovery of "black gold" in the Arctic—a giant, 9.6-billion-barrel oil find at Prudhoe Bay on the North Slope. Such a massive economic impact on the state—including construction of the trans-Alaska oil pipeline and billions of tax revenue dollars consequently cascading into the state treasury—could only accelerate the rate of cultural change in rural Alaska, especially technologically. Today, for instance, jets carry cargo and passengers daily to Kotzebue, which remains the trade and transportation hub for some six thousand residents in a more than thirty-six thousand-square-mile region as big as the state of Indiana. In the modern era, many of Kotzebue's approximately three thousand residents, 85 percent of whom are Iñupiaq Eskimo, enjoy many of the same amenities as other American communities such as electricity, central heating, cable television, telephones, and indoor plumbing. Recently, the local customer-owned and -managed telephone cooperative, OTZ Telephone, opened up to the region access to the information superhighway.

Although the delivery of adequate sanitation and other household comforts lags behind in the smaller rural Alaska communities—villages with populations of just fifty or a few hundred—they typically are connected to the outside world by the nearly universal technologies of telephone and television.

For all the technological and cultural change, though, most of rural Alaska remains distinct from the Lower 48 states, and even from Alaska's urban areas, in one key respect: its geographic isolation is rendered complete by virtue of not being connected by roads to the outside world. Kotzebue's dirt and gravel roads, which snake around one another but scarcely leave the city proper, are covered with clean, wondrously bright snow most of the year. (Each summer those same unpaved thoroughfares can make the entire community annoyingly, even health-threateningly dusty.) Of course, the town's scarce blacktop—other than one main thoroughfare paved for the first time in 1996—automatically confers upon Kotzebue the status of "unusual" in an America that is elsewhere almost universally covered with and connected by hard, smooth streets and highways.

Another unusual feature is that in rural Alaska, the scarcity of roads means that the overland trails and lakes, rivers, and coastal waters typically serve as each region's primary "highways."

Kotzebue, for example, is accessible only by aircraft, snowmobile, and dog team in winter.

Despite the similarities of travel and technology that bind communities together in rural Alaska (sometimes called the "bush"), the scenery surrounding these human outposts encompasses vast differences. They include the majestic peaks of the Brooks Range that splay east–west across the upper tier of the state, to the spruce- and birch-lined rolling hills, lofty peaks, valleys, and river-beds of Alaska's Interior, to the vast stretches of treeless tundra along the northern and western coasts that for much of the year are covered with meringuelike, hard-packed snow.

In December, the sun disappears below the horizon and "darkness" officially descends upon the arctic. This notion of a lack of light creates a mistakenly grim picture of a truly glorious winter. Here, during the clearer, colder days, the arctic's particular beauty becomes especially distinct at twilight (in the afternoon!), as the stars present themselves in an almost neon-blue sky rimmed with a salmon-pink horizon. On some evenings, the moon's bright reflection on the brilliantly white snow creates an illusion, as if the snowdrifts were emanating light of their own. Even with a waning moon, the aurora borealis, also known as the northern lights, brings light to the sky—multicolored, moving, shimmering, dancing light! Indeed, winter visitors to the arctic are often surprised to find that Alaska's arctic actually can offer more light than dark.

At the same time, winter in Kotzebue also can cause temperatures to plummet to 50 degrees below zero, and even lower upriver. Kotzebue, exposed as it is to the frozen ocean on the windswept coast, has recorded windchills to 100 degrees below zero and even lower. That's cold! But a favorite qualifier of those who live in the arctic is, "Yeah, but it's a dry cold," the implication being that the arctic may actually feel warmer than a damp place such as New England or, say, much of northern Europe.

Things do warm up during the arctic's fleeting summer season, however, when small boats ply regional waters and barges out of Seattle deliver fuel, equipment, and other supplies to Kotzebue and its surrounding camps and villages for the long winter season.

The remoteness and sparse human habitation of rural Alaska also mean that many Alaska Native residents, who mostly were not involuntarily removed from their ancestral homelands like Native Americans in the Lower 48, can still maintain strong ties to their

traditional hunting and gathering cultures, pursuing the seasonal harvests of wild food that include berries, caribou, moose, salmon and other fish species, beluga whales, seals, muskrat, bear, ducks, and geese.

As for the cash economy, in the Kotzebue area, in addition to employment opportunities in government agencies and the local service industry, residents of Northwest Alaska also operate a small commercial fishing fleet alongside their annual subsistence salmon harvest and host up to twelve thousand tourists a year through an enterprise run by NANA, the local Native regional corporation. Passage of the Alaska Native Claims Settlement Act in 1971, a landmark piece of congressional legislation attempting to resolve Alaska Native land claims, created thirteen Native regional corporations such as NANA and more than two hundred village corporations. These corporations were established to provide Natives legal claim to their lands and to provide a mechanism for stewardship over Native lands as well as for social and economic development. Shareholders in NANA also may work at its Red Dog Mine north of Kotzebue, excavating one of the world's largest lead and zinc deposits in a joint venture with a Canadian firm.

Facing page, top: Kotzebue, Alaska. This coastal hub community (pop. 3,004), which serves ten smaller villages in northwestern Alaska, lies thirty miles above the Arctic Circle. Photo by Jim Magdanz.

Facing page, bottom: Front Street is Kotzebue's "Main Street" with two general/grocery stores, two restaurants, several video outlets, a hotel and the post office. Photo by John Creed.

Despite this and other considerable economic development throughout rural Alaska in recent decades, rural unemployment is far higher than in the state's major urban centers of Anchorage, Fairbanks, and Juneau. Nevertheless, the vast majority of the state's prosperity does not come from its three largest cities. Without a doubt, the capital driving Alaska's economy emanates from rural Alaska's natural resource wealth. From the North Slope oil fields to Interior coal mines to coastal commercial fishing to Red Dog's world-class mineral deposits, rural Alaska creates the wealth that benefits all state residents.

One of the significant improvements for rural Alaskans, access to higher education, arrived in the 1970s, particularly after the state treasury began to overflow with revenue from development activities related to the gargantuan North Slope oil fields. Native and rural leaders worked with the University of Alaska to establish community colleges, which today have become branch campuses of Alaska's urban universities throughout rural Alaska. One such 1970s creation was Chukchi Community College in Kotzebue, which in 1987 became a branch campus of the University of Alaska Fairbanks. At Chukchi College this anthology came into being.

Unfortunately, as the state oil revenues shrink with North Slope oil reserves, some urban legislators have steadily mounted pressure to close the university's extended rural campuses. That threat is real. With the bulk of state legislative power vested in the mostly non-Native population base of Alaska's urban areas, Alaska Natives living in less populous rural areas typically see their funding in all services cut first—perhaps a contemporary extension of broken promises and treaties experienced in the Lower 48.

Some urban legislators have stated that if rural residents wanted a college education, they should "come to the cities to get it." But in the absence of higher education locally, many rural students could not attend college, for this would mean giving up leadership roles and key jobs in their small communities, leaving behind their families as well as subsistence activities that sustain them. In some cases, newer technologies may be able to bring urban and rural educational interests closer together, but past experience has demonstrated that courses "beamed" into rural Alaska from the urban centers do not have the same success as those taught by faculty who live in the communities they serve. In addition, there is always a danger in assuming that the transmission of knowledge should flow primarily (or only) in one direction: from urban to rural.

So narrow a view would follow a long tradition of the dominant society's disrespect for or ignorance of Native people's more than ten-thousand-year track record of successful, if challenging, life in the Far North. Indeed, like the history of Native Americans in the Lower 48, not all changes rolling into rural Alaska have been positive.

From the initial contact with outsiders, diseases ripped through Native populations with no immunities to such maladies. The influx of outsiders established new governance and commerce that, when not ignoring Native peoples, in some instances enslaved and slaughtered them, as the Russians did to the Aleuts during a colonial occupation that began in 1741. After the United States purchased Alaska in 1867, disregard for and discrimination against Alaska Natives continued, including denying them citizenship until 1924 and maintaining legal segregation against Natives, which was not abolished by Alaska's territorial legislature until the mid-1940s.

In the nineteenth century, when the Russians were still colonizing Alaska, Yankee whalers from New England hunted extensively in arctic waters. These Yankee whalers brutalized many of the Native peoples they encountered, while driving the arctic's whale population, on which the coastal Iñupiat depended, to near extinction. In addition to new diseases, the New England whalers also introduced alcohol to Natives who had no previous experience with this addictive drug.

Throughout territorial days beginning in 1867 and escalating with the federal government's granting of statehood to Alaska in 1959, white settlers, usually with the full support and encouragement of the government, have continued to encroach on Native lands as these outsiders sought a new life and their piece of Alaska's extraordinary wealth. Perhaps the most divisive issue in Alaska today remains the unresolved issue of how to manage limited fish and game resources to assure Native and rural residents their right to continue subsistence hunting and fishing while accommodating other commercial and sport hunting and fishing interests.

Over the past century, Euro-American society also has brought its own brand of spirituality to rural Alaska. For example, missionaries of the Friends Church, arriving in Kotzebue in 1897, introduced to local people a Western religion that forbade traditional Eskimo singing and dancing, an ancient pursuit these Christian missionaries both feared and considered evil, pagan, and "shamanistic." While this caused much of traditional spirituality to be lost or shrouded in shame, some Elders today still recollect a sense of fear about the past because of the potential for shamans to abuse their power.

In addition, the church did bring comfort to people as they watched in disbelief as massive numbers of their kin died of previously unknown diseases such as influenza and smallpox. According to Yup'ik writer Harold Napoleon from Hooper Bay, Alaska, the survivors were "born into shock. They woke to a world in shambles, many of their people and their beliefs strewn around them, dead. In their minds they had been overcome by evil. Their medicines and their medicine men and women had proven useless. Everything they had believed in had failed. Their ancient world had collapsed" (Yuuyaraq: The Way of the Human Being, ed. Eric Madsen, Center for Cross-Cultural Studies, College of Rural Alaska, University of Alaska Fairbanks, 1991, p. 11).

In the last decade, Christian denominations in Alaska have pub-

licly apologized for their unjust treatment of Native peoples in previous times. The resistance of the Friends Church to Eskimo dancing and singing has softened somewhat in recent years, but after
decades of internalizing such a stigma, some Native people still
have difficulty embracing this part of their cultural legacy.

Likewise, the legacy of government-sponsored educational institutions is marred by policies and actions blindly allegiant to Western change in the government's quest to "civilize" Alaska Natives.
In particular, the loss of Native languages began with early educators, who banned Native languages in school and beat students for
daring to speak their own language, a policy first exacted upon Indian tribes in the Lower 48 and continued in Alaska. (Omnipresent
television today nearly drowns out the efforts of local schools and
publicly funded radio stations to keep traditional languages alive.
The strongest antidote to language loss, like everywhere else, remains the older generations speaking their language to their children at home.)

But rather than scapegoat this country's past—remaining stuck
in the especially shameful 1800s when policies of the United States
military, civilians, and official government all but wiped out Native
American tribes—we can find similar policies and actions, if less
overt ones, enduring well into the latter half of the twentieth century in the Far North. In Alaska, perhaps the quintessential example of how non-Natives have trampled over Native people's
rights in the name of Western progress can be found right in
Kotzebue's own backyard. In the late 1950s and early 1960s, the
federal government and nuclear scientist Edward Teller pushed
Project Chariot, an unbelievable scheme by the U.S. Atomic Energy
Commission to create a deep-water harbor along the arctic coast
just north of Kotzebue by detonating up to six thermonuclear
bombs.

A nuclear blast of this magnitude would have struck in the middle
of the Eskimos' ancestral lands and waterways from which they
have continued to sustain their way of life for centuries. Alaska's
most powerful institutions—the church, press, chambers of commerce, higher education, legislature, and so forth—enthusiasti-
cally backed this scheme with little regard for, let alone input from,
Natives living near the proposed blast site. In fact, even the administration of the University of Alaska at the time was urging federal
officials to move ahead with the atomic blasts. Had they gone off,

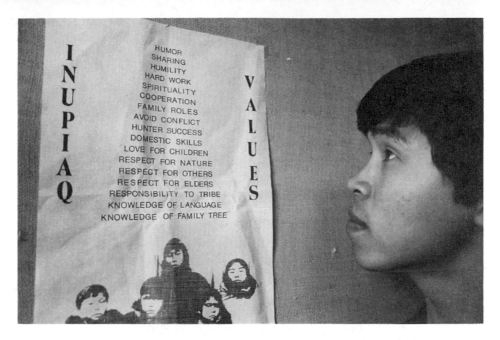

INUPIAQ VALUES

HUMOR
SHARING
HUMILITY
HARD WORK
SPIRITUALITY
COOPERATION
FAMILY ROLES
AVOID CONFLICT
HUNTER SUCCESS
DOMESTIC SKILLS
LOVE FOR CHILDREN
RESPECT FOR NATURE
RESPECT FOR OTHERS
RESPECT FOR ELDERS
RESPONSIBILITY TO TRIBE
KNOWLEDGE OF LANGUAGE
KNOWLEDGE OF FAMILY TREE

Iñupiaq Jason Jessup of Kotzebue looks at poster listing Iñupiaq values, which were identified as part of the Iñupiat Ilitqusiat (Eskimo Spirit) movement in the early 1980s in the NANA Region, which includes Kotzebue and ten outlying villages in Northwest Alaska. Eugene, Oregon, 1983. Photo by John Creed.

they were estimated to have been some 160 times more powerful than the atomic bomb dropped on Hiroshima at the end of World War II in 1945, according to Fairbanks author Dan O'Neill in *The Firecracker Boys* (New York: St. Martin's Press, 1994, p. 41).

Meanwhile, the Iñupiat themselves, with help from a small band of committed conservationists and dissidents in Fairbanks and nationwide, eventually alerted the nation and stopped Project Chariot.

Alaska's mainstream press, particularly the *Fairbanks Daily News-Miner* and the *Anchorage Daily Times*, also had been championing Project Chariot while ignoring opposition, so in 1961 Natives started their own newspaper, the *Tundra Times*. Led by the late Iñupiaq artist and crusading publisher/editor Howard Rock, the paper helped spawn Native unity as well as political activism that helped pressure the U.S. Congress to pass the Alaska Native Claims Settlement Act of 1971. (Nevertheless, Native representation in the Alaska press today remains minuscule. Natives make up nearly 17 percent of the state's six hundred thousand-plus population, yet represent less than 1 percent of the state's journalists.) The land claims act granted Natives title to 44 million acres of land, and for lands lost in the settlement, Natives received $962.5 million to establish 13 Native regional corporations and 206 village corporations.

Despite the federal government's recognition of aboriginal land rights in Alaska in 1971, an ongoing litany of cultural destruction arising from outsider contact has had devastating impacts on Alaska's indigenous population, with ill physical and mental health among Alaska Native people persisting into the modern era. Pressures that contribute to the abuse of alcohol, of illegal drugs, and of tobacco—and even over-consumption of soda pop and other chemical-laden, empty calorie junk food—in turn contribute to escalating, unprecedented rates of cancer, heart disease, diabetes, and other chronic diseases as well as premature death from preventable illness, accidents, homicide, suicide, and domestic violence.

Despite the tragic consequences of this history, however, Alaska Natives have survived, even prevailed. Today, many Natives are finding success in a newly structured cross-cultural world where, as one Iñupiaq Elder in her wisdom has observed, Natives are discovering how to "walk in two worlds with one spirit."

As an example of one way to help bridge these two worlds, today many Alaska Natives are becoming schoolteachers, Native corporation leaders, social workers, and other needed professionals, all in their own communities. Many are able to move into these positions as a result of pursuing higher education at the rural campuses of the University of Alaska and elsewhere.

Education is just one of many avenues for Natives to arrive at a safe crossroads between themselves and Western culture. Another example would be the study and incorporation of the Iñupiat Ilitqusiat values of humor, sharing, humility, hard work, spirituality, cooperation, family roles, avoidance of conflict, hunter success, domestic skills, love for children, respect for nature, respect for others, respect for Elders, responsibility to tribe, knowledge of language, and knowledge of family tree. These values can be successfully dovetailed with Western culture. For example, through the often challenging process of discovery that students undergo in writing, they appreciate the meaning of hard work.

Also, through the sharing of the most uplifting examples of Western arts, literature, and sciences, and through respectful contact with positive, non-Native teachers, students can find qualities of Western culture to admire and to incorporate in their own psyches. Likewise, Native teachers who have been schooled in Western institutions as well as at tribal colleges can share a positive link between the two cultures.

Today Chukchi College delivers academic courses not only to Kotzebue and its ten surrounding Iñupiaq villages, but in partnership with its sister campuses, Chukchi serves up to 160 or more communities across the vast reaches of rural Alaska. Faculty members conduct classes through satellite-assisted audioconference and video-instructional materials in order to reach communities as distant as the Aleutians and as remote as Barrow in the extreme north, plus scores of villages in between. Student assignments move by fax machine or computer e-mail.

Within this context, writings for this anthology began during the 1987-88 school year through a University of Alaska student writing project called Chukchi News and Information Service, which publishes essays, news stories, and other informational or opinion pieces in newspapers and magazines across Alaska. This approach to publishing student writing differs from most others nationwide because we were not creating our own magazine or newspaper. Rather, this approach finds a place for student writing in the existing print media, and mostly the mainstream print media at that.

By 1993, Chukchi News and Information Service had become a regular feature in the *Anchorage Daily News*, Alaska's largest and most influential newspaper, where Chukchi students were able to communicate their world view with the tens of thousands of fellow Alaskans statewide on a regular basis.

With the Chukchi News and Information Service project in operation for a decade, the logical next step was to create a permanent collection of the most compelling and "book-adaptable" pieces. Thus, this anthology comes from nontraditional, generally older students who are Iñupiaq, Yup'ik, or Siberian Yup'ik Eskimos or Athabascan Indians who hail from either the larger hub communities such as Kotzebue and Nome or from smaller villages such as Emmonak in Southwest Alaska or Northway on the Canadian border.

Through the Chukchi News and Information Service writing project, we have sought a wider audience than just fellow students and professors. Native students write of childhoods spent traveling across the arctic wilderness by dog team, following the ancient traditions of their forebears, pursuing fish and game, and moving from one seasonal camp to the next. Their pieces bear witness to a unique way of life that is undergoing sweeping changes in their own lifetimes.

Their upbringing hearkens back to a hunting-and-gathering way of life more strongly grounded in a subsistence economy than one based on cash. And while the balance had tipped more heavily toward a cash economy by the end of the twentieth century, these writers' subsistence practices, which inherently bind the practitioner to the land, remain the very core of their existence. This often is true even for those who have had to relearn subsistence lifeways, if they were raised elsewhere or somehow missed out on subsistence camp experiences growing up. For many, the relationship to the land remains foremost.

The majority of these students' writing fits into what is known as "cultural journalism," where the ordinary way of life receives the attention, not the unusual or extraordinary events covered in straight news pieces, and where this reflection of the ordinary fabric of life also can instruct and offer profound insight.

Many writers who publish through Chukchi News and Information Service learned English as their second language, if they grew up speaking their Native tongue, such as central Yup'ik, the language of the Eskimos of Southwest Alaska. Also, many Native students find standard written English a particularly challenging task as a result of having grown up around "village" English, a form of local English common in rural Alaska.

In fact, most who publish through Chukchi News and Information Service come into class as novice writers in basic skill-building classes. Although a handful of writers do hold degrees or wrote their pieces in advanced journalism courses, the majority of the pieces in this book were written by developmental, first-, or second-year college students working toward an associate's degree.

This should be considered a strength, not a weakness, which creates an authentic voice that truly reflects "real" people—that is, mature adults with extensive experience in the real world.

Finally, what makes the writing in this book different from that of most books about Alaska Natives is that the writing emanates from a group of people rather than a solo author. While authorship of books generally follows in the Western tradition that promotes individual achievement, Native culture traditionally has shown greater reverence for the consciousness of the group.

For this reason, we believe that rather than a single voice, a multitude of authentic voices originating in rural Alaska can author a uniquely accurate and compelling statement of this special land and people, and in doing so help shape the history of Alaska on the cusp of a new century.

NOTES

1. The Iñupiat means "the real people" and is used as a noun to identify the Eskimos that live primarily in the Northwest and North Slope regions of Alaska. "Iñupiaq" is used throughout this text as an adjective. Iñupiaq also is the name of the language. The term "Eskimo" is used frequently in rural Alaska generally without negative connotations, while, in contrast, the term "Inuit" is preferred in Canada. In Kotzebue, for example, the post office is housed in what is known as the Eskimo Building. However, the generic term "Eskimo" does not distinguish a Yup'ik from a Iñupiaq, which makes it a less useful term.

Similarly, the term "Indian" is used in Alaska but, again, the specific names of Native groups such as Athabascan or Tlingit are more useful. Even more precise, within the Athabascan, specific subgroups often are referred to, such as the Gwich'in or the Dena'ina.

The terms "Native" and "Alaska Native" are used to refer broadly to all of Alaska's indigenous peoples—the Eskimos, Indians, and Aleuts—or to any individual belonging to one of these peoples.

2. "Alaska Native" is the proper name for the indigenous people of Alaska collectively. Athabascan Indians live mainly in Interior Alaska; Tlingit, Tsimshian, and Haida Indians in Southeast Alaska; Yup'ik Eskimos in Southwest Alaska, with Siberian Yup'iks on St. Lawrence Island ; Iñupiaq Eskimos in Northwest Alaska and on the North Slope; and Aleuts along the Aleutian Islands.

Authentic Alaska

Red Dog
Kivalina   Mine
Noatak   **Iñupiat**
Little   Kiana
Diomede I.   Kotzebue
      Selawik
Siberian   Deering
Yup'ik   Elim
     Nome   Rampart
      Unalakleet   Fairbanks
Gambell   Emmonak   **Athabascan**
Savoonga   St. Michael   Northway

Yup'ik
   Anchorage

       Juneau

Aleut   **Tlingit**

     0   300 km   **Haida**
     0   200 mi   **Tsimshian**

ALASKA NATIVE PEOPLES

Map showing the traditional areas of settlement of Alaska Native peoples. The "boundaries" typically are blurred, partcularly today because of the movement of Native people to various parts of the state, including to Alaska's largest "village," Anchorage.

I

Autobiography

My Parents Lived a wandering life, for did all the Indians at Mohegan,
they Chiefly Depended upon Hunting, Fishing, & Fowling for their Living.
—SAMSON OCCOM, Mohegan Indian, September 17, 1768

Rural Alaska spans America's last great expanse of wild territory. Scattered across this sparsely populated land are relatively large and small, predominantly Alaska Native villages, clinging to the coast of Alaska or nestled along the inland river systems.

These remote villages form the backdrop for this chapter's short life stories, which reveal the cultural diversity, originality, and endurance characteristic of rural Alaska Natives. Remarkably, not long ago Native people still lived almost completely from the land in rural Alaska. Even someone the age of the first writer, Iñupiaq Dollie Hawley, born in the mid-1950s, was raised "the old way," speaking her Native language. Indeed, Iñupiaq Tina Jones was still migrating with the seasons well into the 1980s, until her family grew so large that constant travel became too much of a strain. In reading the work of young contributor Spencer Rearden, one is reassured that the tradition of a close relationship to the land will continue in future generations.

Other Natives leave rural Alaska to serve in the military, such as James Gooden, who writes about the hardship of adjusting to mainstream America and, not surprisingly, warmer climates. On a deeper level, joining the service requires a great sacrifice because it means leaving behind small communities and families so very far away. Conversely, others such as Mildred Savok look forward to the opportunity to travel Outside. (Outside with a capital "O" means someplace other than Alaska.)

Kathleen Sherman reveals a work ethic that drives her to be self-sufficient in the working world while holding fast to traditional activities and values. Julia Stalker explores the important lessons learned from her rich heritage, particularly from her grandparents who taught her skills, discipline, and values.

Hannah Paniyavluk Loon is an Iñupiaq writer especially noted for her humor, which buoys her as she balances many responsibilities in both worlds, such as working full-time in Kotzebue and raising a family, while also making time for subsistence hunting, fishing, and gathering. Alaska Native students often inject an idiomatic sense of humor in their writing, which is subtle and more likely to elicit a chuckle than a knee-slapping guffaw.

Finally, Yup'ik Lucy Daniels "can still hear the swish, swish, swish of the paddle as Grandma guided the canoe over placid waters" when Lucy was growing up, "in a time that now seems like ancient Alaska."

Growing Up in Kivalina on Alaska's Remote Arctic Coast

Dollie Ahyahlooktook Hawley   Iñupiaq   Kotzebue

•Kotzebue

My name is Dollie Ahyahlooktook Kodine Hawley. I was born on March 18, 1955, at Kivalina, an Iñupiaq Eskimo community on Alaska's arctic coast.

Today, Kivalina has a population of about three hundred people. My parents, Robert Tovaruk and Sarah Negruklook Hawley, brought me up, along with the help of my grandma, Myra Ahquruk Hawley, who died in the 1960s, and my four aunts and uncles, who all resided at Kivalina, although some have since passed away.

My childhood was full of tough days—that I can tell you. I remember my mother trying to raise money to buy her three sons and six daughters rummage sale clothes for school or just for everyday wear. Two of my sisters passed away in the mid-1960s, one at birth and the other at about eight months. The latter was buried in Anchorage because my family had no money to send for her body. One younger sister was given away for adoption in the 1960s to a family who resides in Kotzebue.

I remember the dark cold days of my youth when my mother would wake us up for school. My dad would light the drum stove with seal-oil blubber to get the fire going. It sure was not an automatic world we lived in, and in those days, it seemed as if life

would stay the same forever. Kivalina always seemed to have very
hard, harsh, and cold weather.

To provide our daily meals, somehow my dad would hitch his
dog sled each winter day with about fourteen or fewer dogs to go
out and hunt the game. Subsistence hunting was very common in
Kivalina in those days. I remember helping my dad by holding the
lantern for him whenever he came home from hunting. He would
leave during the early dawn and come home late at night. Never
would he arrive back home at midday. Most of the time, he would
return to the village with a sled load of subsistence food—our meal
for the day. My grandma, Myra, made good use of the game. She
would use seal oil for all sorts of medicines, especially when we
had bad colds or the flu. When we were sick, my grandma would
make us swallow a teaspoon or two of seal oil, three times daily,
just as a doctor would prescribe something to us. The only
difference was that this was seal oil and not prescription drugs
from a modern pharmacy.

I found the grade school I attended in Kivalina to be hard and
complicated at first. I spoke the Iñupiaq language that had been
taught to me by my parents, aunts, uncles, grandma Myra, and all
the Elders who lived in my village. I remember the teacher forbid-

ding us to use the Iñupiaq that we had spoken daily. Instead, we were taught the English language. It was hard and heavy for me to catch on to the alphabet and the numbers, but I somehow finally caught on using English in class.

I can also remember the teacher teaching us our manners, such as saying, "Please," "May I?" or "Excuse me" and "Thank you." She also taught us not to slurp whenever we ate our meals. Slurping was a very big problem in those days.

Thanks to God we all learned not to slurp.

Iñupiaq Grows Up
Traveling with the Seasons

Tina Maria Jones   Iñupiaq   Kotzebue

I, Tina Maria Harris Jones, was born in Kotzebue, Alaska, on November 1, 1962. I was adopted by my maternal grandparents at birth. I never knew I was adopted until I got older, so I always assumed that "Mom and Pop" were my real parents.

During childhood, I grew up at different camps, living a subsistence way of life. I was the youngest in our family, so I guess I was pretty spoiled growing up. As I got older, I helped my father and brother commercial fish for salmon in Kotzebue Sound every summer. We never caught much, but we did manage to sell enough fish to buy supplies for the winter.

The only transportation we had in those days was our dog team, which I helped my father take care of, including feeding and hitching them up whenever we were going somewhere. We had both a winter camp and summer camp that we moved to as the seasons changed. My favorite time of year was spring, when I got to go duck hunting. Most of the time I went by myself, but sometimes the guys would take me when they got tired of hearing me beg.

I remember setting squirrel traps every summer by the lagoon in Sisualik, a traditional camp twelve miles across the sound from Kotzebue and where we later settled down and built a house. I caught a lot of squirrels every summer. In fact, Mom promised she would sew up a squirrel parkie for my first-born daughter someday.

Kivalina, Alaska, 1993. This coastal community (pop. 372) is located ninety miles north of Kotzebue. In recent years, plans have called for relocating the village due to sea erosion. Photo by Jim Magdanz.

Sisualik, Alaska, 1993. Sisualik is located across the Kotzebue Sound from Kotzebue in northwestern arctic Alaska and serves primarily as a site for summer subsistence camps. Photo by Jim Magdanz.

*A Native allotment refers to lands transferred to individual Natives under the 1887 General Allotment Act, also known as the Dawes Act, which enabled the government to impose 160-acre deeds on Native Americans (rather than lands being held communally). While this act was designed initially for the Lower 48, some Alaska Natives later successfully filed for allotments.

It was a laugh then, because I told her I would never have any kids, but I guess she knew different. Today I'm the mother of eight children. Mom never got around to sewing that parkie, but I know she really wanted to.

I remember the cool fall nights when all the kids would get together and play kick-the-can in the bushes behind our house. Those were scary times for me, I guess because I was very young. The big boys would try to scare us little kids. The neighbors were all family: aunts, uncles, and their kids. In fact, we were like one big family.

To pass the time on the long winter nights, my mom would teach me how to scrape caribou skins to make mukluks [traditional-style boots made of sealskin, caribou legskin or calfskin]. Those were tiring times, mostly because I was lazy and didn't want to do it. I learned how to sew when I was very young. It cost me a lot of poked fingers, but I kept on with it. I'm very thankful today that I did, for it's a skill I will never forget.

I remember the spring days when the beluga were sighted way out in the ocean. The Elders would make sure that everyone was very quiet. They claimed that the beluga could hear from great distances. We would sit on the beach and watch the boats go out after them. When they caught a beluga, all the people would get together as a team and pull the beluga out of the water. Everyone who participated would share in the eating of the flippers.

The fall days were filled with picking berries. We picked blackberries in our backyard, but we had to go by boat to find salmonberries and blueberries. I haven't gone anywhere in years to pick berries, and so those are things I never have taught my children.

I left home when I was fifteen years of age and traveled around to different villages. I married at eighteen. My husband and I moved to various camps also, just like I had done with my family. In fact, our first child was born on the first day of spring at camp in my in-laws' home. My husband and mother-in-law helped deliver him. It was too stormy to bring a doctor in from Kotzebue. At that time, I really didn't know what I was getting into, though it was a great experience for us all. As time went by, though, it became harder and harder for us to move from camp to camp, as I gave birth to a new baby almost every year.

In 1983, my husband, his brothers, and I built our house on my mother's Native allotment eleven miles north of Kotzebue.* Although we settled down for a while, come spring, we moved on to our summer camp. Those were the best times we had back then. We swam most of the summer, and the six kids we'd had by then really enjoyed it.

Not everything went perfectly, however. In the summer of 1987 at our summer camp, our six-month-old baby boy died suddenly during the night from pneumonia. Since then, the feeling I had for that camp has never been the same. To this day, we never have returned.

In the fall of 1988, after the commercial fishing season was over, my family and I packed up and boated far up the Kobuk River. Our destination was my brother-in-law's camp about twenty miles upriver from tiny, remote Kobuk. We stayed almost until freeze-up, but we were living in a tent and it had gotten very cold, so the four youngest kids and I then moved to the village of Kobuk. We lived in Kobuk until February 1991, when my family and I moved to Kotzebue. We know Kobuk to be our home, however, and will someday return.

Waterfowl Hunter's Dream Pursued by Family

•Kotzebue

Spencer Rearden   *Yup'ik*   *Kotzebue*

My family always has been an outdoor family. Every one of us loves to go camping. My mom enjoys picking berries, and my dad loves to fly. To me, going camping and being in the outdoors is a vacation, except that I don't relax. I'm either alert and active—or exhausted and asleep.

I was born in Kodiak, Alaska, in 1979. I don't know much about Kodiak, because that year we moved to Fairbanks so my parents could finish college. In 1980 both of my parents completed their degrees. My mom was to become a teacher, and my dad already had accepted a job working for Fish and Wildlife in Bethel, Alaska, where we lived then for eleven years. Bethel is sprawled on the banks of the Kuskokwim River. The area's terrain consists of sand, tundra, and many lakes. Not far from Bethel lies the Yukon-Kuskokwim Delta, where much of the waterfowl in Alaska spend their summers. There I learned how to hunt waterfowl.

As a little kid, I wasn't an angel. I usually tagged along with my brother, Stefan, every place he went. I always sneaked away to play, and by the time I came home, I would be filthy. My parents said that after I took a bath, a trail of dirt and sand would lead to the drain. One day Stefan went off to play without me. My mom told me to stay inside because it was my nap time. Of course I didn't listen. I wanted to find adventure with my brother. I went to look for him. My mom became worried and asked my dad to go search for me. When he found me, I was asleep in the middle of the road with my face in the dirt and my butt up in the air.

My family's outdoor life involves commercial fishing. We own a permit for the Yukon River. When I turned seven, my parents started taking my brother and me out commercial fishing. When we fished twenty-four-hour periods, which means fishing all day and night, I always fell asleep in the wooden, open skiff wrapped up in a plastic tarp, despite the boat's rocking and the cold. Sometimes we saw spots of snow on the riverbank, sagging into the current. Now that I am older, my dad lets me fish with just my mom. From commercial fishing, I'm saving money for college.

My hunger to seek adventure grew. I began exploring behind our house, which is open country. I became fascinated with the ducks I saw on the lakes. Sometimes my fascination with waterfowl and new country drove me farther and farther. By the time I came home, I felt I'd stumbled over tundra for a hundred miles.

My dad began taking me out hunting when I was six years old. Our first trip together was duck hunting up the Napakiak Slough, which is twenty miles from Bethel. Stefan and my dad shot some ducks, but I was too young to handle a shotgun properly. I was so amazed by these birds that I also wanted to get a duck. I begged and begged until finally my dad showed me a young teal swimming along shore unaware of us. I was so excited I missed the first shot. The second shot hit the bird, and I got my first duck. This was the first of many adventures waterfowl hunting.

A year or two later in the fall, my dad flew all of us in our airplane to a place called Pike Lake. Good marsh and waterfowl are plentiful there. We stayed in a run-down cabin, but it was convenient, for it was close to the marsh. I had a 20-gauge shotgun that I had never used before. When we approached the marsh through the woods, we saw a whole flock of white-fronted geese grazing. I remember their language of loud clucks. We closed in on them. For every step taken, it seemed a twig would break. My brother and I stayed behind and watched my dad flush the birds and drop two white-fronts. Watching the big birds drop to the water thrilled me like watching fireworks fall from the sky.

On that trip, I remember feeling the absence of our retriever, Smoky, who died the year before. Hunting with a dog is half the fun.

The next day not many birds were flying, so my dad told me to shoot some ducks that were minding their own business feeding. I had to trudge in mud halfway up to my knees to get close enough for a shot. I wanted to show my dad I could get a duck by myself. When I got in range, I fired my gun, and from the unexpected kick I fell in the mud. That got me a duck and several laughs.

My dad has taught me a lot about hunting. He has shown me how and where to set decoys, how to handle the dog and the advantages of a dog, and most of all how to have fun even if we didn't get anything.

I love being out in the marsh feeling free. But I would have to leave the marshes for different country unfamiliar to me, for my dad accepted a job in Kotzebue when I was in the seventh grade.

This northwestern region of Alaska is rich with animals and stunning scenery. There are bare rocky mountains, spruce trees, and rolling valleys full of things to do. The mountains look like paintings to me. I had never seen mountains so bold and so close until I moved here. I enjoy the country and animals we hunt, but caribou hunting is not as exciting as waterfowl hunting. To me, nothing is better than being out in the marsh.

Today, I am training a young Labrador retriever, also named Smoky, for my companion out in the marsh and, of course, to fetch my birds. Training and caring for Smoky has made me very attached to her. I plan to bring my dog with me when I leave home for college, but if I can't, I hope my little brother, Sterling, will take my place in further educating Smoky and keeping my family's outdoor legacy alive.

Life's Journey Around the Country and Back to Kiana

James Gooden   Iñupiaq   Kiana

My name is James Ronald Gooden. I was born on July 14, 1946. My real given name at birth was Ronald Andrews Tobuk. I was born in Fairbanks, Alaska, at the former St. Joseph's Memorial Hospital.

My two older sisters and I, though, were culturally adopted at very young ages by three sisters in the northwestern region of Alaska. Cultural adoption means being adopted by other family members or by kinship within the same tribe. At the time, I was about six months old. All of us children were a year apart.

I was adopted by Samuel and Pauline Gooden of Kiana. My next older sister was adopted by Archie and Hadley Ferguson of Kotzebue. My oldest sister, when she was four or five years old, was adopted to Edward and Nora Norton of Selawik, Alaska.

My new family and I lived in Kiana for about a year, then moved to Selawik, where my dad worked as a longshoreman for a couple years. At about the age of five, my dad moved us to Fairbanks where he got a job as a janitor, in 1952, at Ladd Air Force Base (now called Fort Wainwright Army Base).

In Fairbanks, I attended several elementary schools until the summer of 1962, when I moved to Kotzebue where I lived with my aunt. In Kotzebue, I attended the eighth grade at the Bureau of Indian Affairs–operated Kotzebue Day School. My adoptive parents, sisters, and brother stayed in Fairbanks and continued to work.

In 1963, I was accepted to attend high school at the Bureau of Indian Affairs Chemawa Indian School, located five miles north of Salem, Oregon. I attended Chemawa for four years and graduated on May 20, 1967.

After graduation, I returned to Fairbanks to be with my mother and father for summer vacation, before leaving again to attend a two-year vocational school. While in Fairbanks that summer, my brother-in-law got me a job with the Alaska Railroad as a laborer, where he worked. I worked for a couple of months until it was time to leave again.

In August 1967, I departed Fairbanks once again, leaving my family to attend the two-year junior college program at the B.I.A.-operated Haskell Institute in Lawrence, Kansas. I studied automotive mechanics. I worked the last five months before graduation for Phillips 66. I returned to Fairbanks after graduation, in May 1969.

Instead of looking for a job as planned, I spent most of my time at home with Mom and Dad. The following June, I received my draft notice for the military and traveled to Anchorage for the physical and evaluation test. The military personnel used tough scare tactics on us. My nephew Richard and I dropped our pencils on the desk and went to the nearest Navy Recruiting Center and joined. We were on their six-month delay program, so this gave us some extra time at home.

December 10, 1969, arrived and I was standing in line, holding a uniform in my arms, sporting the traditional haircut, with men hollering in my ears. I was in the United States Navy to fulfill my six-year obligation. Boot camp ended the following March 1970, and I departed for home for two weeks leave.

I spent most of my time again with Mom and Dad. Although I sensed that time was short, little did I know that this would be the last time I would spend with my Dad. After my two weeks were up, I returned to San Diego Naval Station to attend the Navy's A-1 Hospital Corps School. Close to graduation, I was summoned out of class to report to the American Red Cross office. I was informed that my father had passed away, and the officials wanted to know if I wanted to go home and attend the funeral. To make the difficult part short, I attended the funeral and returned to San Diego.

I put in a request for humanitarian assignment to be stationed in Alaska. My request was denied, and I was transferred to the Naval Air Station in Pensacola, Florida. I worked in the naval hospital and helped care for some of the wounded that came back from Vietnam.

After four requests for a humanitarian assignment in Alaska were denied, despite the family hardship that existed at home, I made my final appeal. I appealed to Alaska's Senator Ted Stevens and explained my situation. My mother had gone through two operations and was beginning to develop heart trouble. She was sixty-five. Her

Kiana, Alaska, 1993.
Kiana (pop. 403) lies
fifty-seven miles to the
east of Kotzebue on the
Kobuk River in north-
western Arctic Alaska.
Photo by Jim Magdanz.

health had gotten worse since Dad's death, and I wanted to take care of her.

Senator Stevens sent a telegram to the Department of the Navy in Washington DC, to release, from active duty, one Hospitalman James Ronald Gooden, service number B932081. In three working days, I was released with an honorable discharge on February 10, 1971.

In Fairbanks, the family decided to take mother back home to the north. My mother, brother, and I moved back to Kiana, where Dad had been buried the year before. After twenty-four years away, we were back home.

I got married in May of 1974 to Emma Mae Morena, the daughter of Leonard and Hilda Morena. I worked at different jobs from Kiana to Kotzebue to the North Slope. My jobs have included being a police officer, a security officer, a magistrate, and a teacher's aide. I enlisted in the Alaska Army National Guard to fulfill my six-year obligation to settle a debt to myself and to the United States Navy. I also owed it to the senator from Alaska who helped me through the red tape. I have now accomplished that. After five years in the Army National Guard, I was honorably discharged.

To date, my wife and I have four healthy children. My mother lived to be seventy-five years old—long enough to see three of the children grow a little. Her favorite was Samuel, whom I named after my father.

Early Lessons Learned
from Grandparents

Julia Jones Anausuk Stalker   Iñupiaq   Kotzebue

I was born in the village of Selawik in 1962. I have five brothers and one sister. We lived in an old log cabin house that we eventually left because it was too cold. We then moved into a tent for the summer, until my dad was done with the new house. My dad built just about all our furniture such as bunk beds, drawers, closets, tables, and chairs.

My parents kept busy looking after all of us. I recall my mother hand sewing clothes for my sister and me. We had red and white dresses, and in front of the collar she sewed red bows to brighten the look. We wore them on special days such as the first day of school and Christmas. Besides all the child-care work, she did laundry, cleaning, and cooking. We didn't have TV then, so instead we spent our time sewing and doing odd jobs in the house. With seven of us kids, our house was crowded, so whenever we were done with our chores, we were sent out to play.

My family moved to Kotzebue in 1975. This would mean transferring from Selawik's small village school to a bigger school. "Can I move in with Aana and Taata for the rest of the school year?" I begged my parents. They talked it over and decided that would be a good idea, but only if my grandparents would take me in. Under one condition I got to stay: I was to abide by all their rules and help out with packing water, doing dishes, and helping Aana with the beaver skins she had prepared for making hats.

I developed a sweet relationship with my grandparents at an early age, especially my grandma. I became attracted to her sewing hobbies. She was very strict when she taught me how to sew. I remember when she repeatedly plucked my sewing needle from my fingers until I held it the right way, and I had to cut the sinu [thread] to a certain length. She used to get so frustrated with me, because it was hard for me to learn. Sometimes I had tears rolling down my face and was scared. It seemed I would never finish my sewing. I found myself looking for something easier to do rather than sewing, but when she noticed my tears, she would smile at me, placing her hand on my shoulder, saying "You will learn, babe."

After I went through the learning stage, Aana handed me material and a beaver skin saying, "You know how now. You make beaver hat for your brother." I sat beside her on the floor as she leaned her back against the couch, humming an old sweet song in Iñupiaq. She and I didn't have much to say to each other as teacher and student. If I did speak, I couldn't say too much other than to answer her in two words. Those words were "yes" and "no." If I said more, I felt as though I was talking back. I was taught never to talk back, especially to Elders. With great respect, I listened to her as she explained in Iñupiaq how to cut the material or skin with a pattern she made. I had to try to understand what she was saying, which I did by watching her motions. To name a few of her creations, she made mukluks, mittens, hats, and parkas.

Every morning my Aana started with a word of prayer and Bible reading. For breakfast she prepared hot sourdough pancakes and fried fresh caribou liver. The kitchen smelled like fried potatoes with onions.

These foods remind me of my fond memories for my late grandfather Taata, my friend. He used to look at me with a smile on his face, knowing that was my favorite meal but that I had to wait till Aana was done reading the Bible before we could eat. When we were done eating at the table, he would test me to see if I learned how to speak or understand Iñupiaq, so whenever he asked me to do him a favor he would ask me in the Iñupiaq language. I couldn't leave until I did the favor exactly how he told me to. I had to memorize the question he asked in Iñupiaq and answer him in Iñupiaq. It wasn't easy. Taata had a look on his face as if a lion were sitting in front of me. This way he knew that once a question was asked, I would answer him correctly. If I made a mistake, he would give me another day. He did not repeat himself.

Also, he was my alarm clock. I'll never forget the feeling when it was time to get up in the morning. His deep hollow voice would scare me out of bed. Loud and clear he'd say, "It's time now. You need to get up one hour before school so that you will have fifteen minutes to walk." (Even though we lived five minutes away from the school.) Today, it's still hard for me to get a "fifteen minute" start. At school recess I used to hurry home to check how far along my Aana's sewing was, because she didn't take long to finish her projects. Smiling at me, her expressions told me that I could do that, too. She taught me to skin caribou, dry the skins, and tan them.

I really didn't have my own choice to go in and out of the house to hang out with my friends whenever I wanted to. I had to obey all her rules.

I realize now that what she taught me is very valuable today. She meant for me to learn so that I could sew for my family when I got married. She taught me enough that I can teach my four children today. I'd rather be sewing among the other things I have to do. I also have had the privilege to teach students how to skin caribou legs at the Kotzebue schools on Iñupiaq days. I'm grateful that my Aana taught me. If I could gain credits for sewing or teaching, I'd give the credits to her, my grandmother, Faye Foster. Thank you, Aana.

Remember Me

Hannah Paniyavluk Loon Iñupiaq Kotzebue

In the month of May when the ice was breaking up, I came into this world and was named after a man called Paniyavluk but never was told why.

I grew up in a reindeer camp called Napaaqtulik, a little ravine northeast of Selawik Lake. In the camp, there was a house I recall where naluaġmiutaq or "whiteman's food" was stored. In the woods, there were other tents, dogs, and trees, as well as children to play with. I remember my parents traveling by dog team during the winter, and I have fond memories of my mother at Napaaqtulik, being a humorous and happy woman, while my father relaxed while smoking Velveteen tobacco. My favorite memory was following Itqilik, my brother, down to the clear, frozen river to hook for grayling. We lay on our stomachs and looked through the ice to watch the fish swimming.

During our early childhood, we were properly clothed with fur

Kotzebue

Selawik, Alaska, 1993. Selawik (pop. 640) is located ninety miles southeast of Kotzebue in north-western Arctic Alaska. The boardwalks across the tundra linking one part of town to another create a distinctive feature of this community. Photo by Jim Magdanz.

and nurtured by my mother. But later, she was constantly in the hospital. An incurable cancer took her life in early fall of 1958, leaving my father, brother, and two sisters. We moved to Selawik where our formal education began and where our grandmother, Nasruluk, took responsibility for our care. Separated from her husband, she lived independently in a little sod house. I recall a year later in the fall, our father once traveled upriver by qayaq [kayak]. He then rafted downriver with logs and rebuilt our grandmother's sod house.

After ice break-up, my brother and I would always follow our grandmother as she ventured off to camp in a little rowboat. Sometimes we rowed the boat or pulled it along the shore, but my favorite was sailing it on lakes. As we sailed, I watched my grandmother enjoy a Camel cigarette and smile as she exhaled the smoke. Oftentimes, I would sneak a cigarette, imitating her way of smoking, but the tobacco was very strong.

I enjoyed my years with grandmother, but in 1962 my brother and I got sent away to boarding school a thousand miles away! I cried the first several nights away from home in this strange environment—Wrangell Institute in southeast Alaska. To me, it was a total culture shock. After that, I went south every fall to attend Mt.

Iñupiaq Hannah
Paniyavluk Loon.
Kotzebue, Alaska,
1992. Photo by
Jim Magdanz.

Edgecumbe High School, also in southeastern Alaska, in Sitka, and returned home each spring. I got used to traveling back and forth. The more time I spent away from home, the less I used the Iñupiaq language. Our language was not Iñupiaq, but "cool man" language. Listening and dancing to rock-'n'-roll music such as Creedence Clearwater Revival, the Beatles, and Percy Sledge was the "in thing." We dressed in the '60s style, including wearing bobby socks. We ratted and sprayed our hair to hold it in style.

We looked forward to going home each spring when school let out in May. As we saw our home village from the plane, some of us got emotional and some got excited. When the villagers at home heard of our arrival, the whole village would rush to the airport to greet us. My grandmother would wait at home. I'd cry when we were reunited because I missed her.

I completed high school in 1969. A man in Selawik asked for my hand in marriage through a letter seeking my father's permission. Luckily, I decided to go to Alaska Methodist University in Anchorage. My father respected my desire.

During my first years of college, I experienced difficulties living an independent life. But I enjoyed cross-country skiing and tumbling, and I met foreign students from Nairobi, Samoa, and Japan, as well as others like me from Alaska.

There was a black, male student from Nairobi who asked me, "If you had to choose between a black man and a white man, which would you marry?" I responded, "Perhaps an Iñupiaq (Eskimo) man." His eyes and teeth gleamed as he laughed at my utterance. Today, I still wonder exactly what he meant.

Much to my surprise, I met a man who came from New Hampshire but whose parents taught in our region of Alaska for many years. We were in the same class: Human Behavioral Sciences. We got married, but he lived in New Hampshire and I lived in Selawik. We could not live together in either world. For a short period, though, we ventured far and wide in Alaska and on the East Coast, which was how I learned how to drive all kinds of cars. Today, I value his friendship and companionship. We separated nicely. He is now remarried and living happily in California.

Nowadays, I enjoy camping and listening to the birds and loons. I like the smell of trees, Labrador tea, and plants budding in early spring. I like to see miniature plants growing on the tundra. Other than listening to and watching nature, there is much work to do at camp, such as getting firewood, checking the nets for fish, picking berries, and riding in my cousin's twelve-foot riverboat with a fifteen-horsepower Evinrude outboard motor.

When I am not at camp, I am independent just like my grandmother, raising four children. I also have spent much time working for the Subsistence Division of the Alaska Department of Fish and Game and the Native regional corporation for Northwest Alaska, NANA. But above all, my biggest reward and joy is returning back to the same spot where our grandmother first raised my brother and me. She is no longer there, but her spirit lives on. And yes, I may light up a cigarette, except now I don't sneak them.

• Kotzebue

Tundra Beckons throughout Life

Kathleen Uhl Sherman   Iñupiaq   Kotzebue

The sun is shining brightly in my eyes as I watch the airplane fly away. As usual, I am spending my summer vacation at Sisualik, my grandparents' summer camp. Soon the plane looks like a dot over the Kotzebue horizon. I slump inside the tent, saddened by the

Historical subsistence from the land: Young woman and child gathering subsistence foods from the tundra, with child in the amaaq position, meaning carried on the mother's back in the traditional way. Alaskan Shepherd Photo Collection, accession number 88-17-15N, in the Elmer E. Rasmuson Library Archives, Alaska and Polar Regions Department, University of Alaska Fairbanks.

thought of being away from my parents, friends, and television. I am seven years old, soon to be eight, and have just completed the second grade.

"Don't be sad. Summer will soon be over and you'll be back home," my grandmother said. I listen to her words and in no time I am no longer lonely.

During my stay at camp, I'd do a lot of outside activities such as berry picking, swimming, and looking for duck eggs in the willows. Now that I am older, I realize that one of the main reasons for my stay at Sisualik was to help my grandmother gather large amounts of berries, blueberries in particular. Sometimes they measured up to the size of my thumb. We walked half a mile or more from camp and found huge blueberry patches and stayed late into the summer evenings. Exhausted at the end of the day, I wouldn't even bother to clean my purple-stained knees. On other days I stuffed the front of my atikłuq with round white shells that later were made into necklaces for my mother and grandmother.

At thirteen, I took my first paid summer job at Rotman's Store as a cashier clerk for eight dollars an hour. I was excited; as long as I was working I'd be able to spend my summer in Kotzebue. My next three summers were spent in Kotzebue as well. No longer was I interested in berry picking and spending numerous hours on the beach picking up shells that the waves had tossed up in a previous night's storm. Now my interests turned toward the latest hairstyles, makeup, and dances. I especially enjoyed spending the money that I had earned during the summer months on clothes, clothes, clothes!

During my high school years, I rarely visited my grandparents in camp. The only time I saw them was during holidays such as Christmas. My family gathered at the Friends Church, which held the largest Christmas program in town. Green and red Christmas ornaments hung from the church's triangle-shaped ceiling. And, as always, a large beautiful tree was wrapped with glittering garlands and glowing lights on the stage where I'd recited my Christmas piece as a young child.

Each year we prepared a huge birthday dinner for my grandmother. She was always happy because she could visit with friends and family. Somehow we managed to comfortably fit everyone into our house. We still have dinners for her, so luckily our house has expanded in size.

After graduation I moved out of my parents' house into a comfortable apartment with my older sister, then later on into one of my own. Responsibilities knocked on my door, and employment was necessary. No longer was I able to spend money and time as freely as I once had. A work schedule had to be followed, and household bills needed to be paid. Yet, somehow I managed, struggling less than I had expected.

I am sitting with my grandmother on the orange autumn tundra, once again picking blueberries. I'm finally spending some time at camp again, during a weekend off from work. Now that I am older, married, and working a full-time job, my time is limited, and I cannot leave whenever I please. Now, I take advantage of every rare opportunity that I have to spend time with my grandparents at their summer or winter camp.

•Kotzebue

My Life As I Remember It

Mildred Aviiksaq Savok   *Iñupiaq*   *Kotzebue*

My mom named me after her mom, including her Eskimo name, Aviiksaq. I was born in Kotzebue, Alaska. My parents were Nellie Gallahorn and Reed Henry, who died in the 1980s, just four days apart. I have two sisters and one brother, Emmett. My sister Pauline is older than me, my sister Shirley younger. Mom had other children who died early in life.

My sister Pauline got married and moved to Casper, Wyoming, in 1963. Today she lives in Arkansas, so we stay in touch by phone.

I remember Grandpa Lester as a kind, caring person. People today tell me he would go to the villages with his boat and bring apples and oranges to the people there. People would tell him to sell them, but he wanted to give them away. I remember Grandpa would take us boating. Unlike other boats, his had a top on it.

When I was nine years old, I started learning to sew on Mom's sewing machine. I made a pair of pants for my nephew. They were too tight, but he wore them anyway. Pauline was proud of what I accomplished at so young an age. My sister and I would play on the pedal, rocking back and forth. I now wished I had kept that old sewing machine so my daughters could see what an old-fashioned sewing machine looked like years ago.

Back in the 1960s, Kotzebue didn't have a high school. Secondary students went away to school after the eighth grade. In springtime, we would meet the plane after school was out for the year. We would go to see who came in and ask them questions about school. In the 1970s, students began attending school in Kotzebue up to the twelfth grade, which disappointed me. I had wanted to go away to attend school, to travel, and to see other cities. I did get that chance, though, when I was accepted for a Job Corps project in Astoria, Oregon. When I was sixteen years old, other village boys and girls and I traveled to Astoria.

In the 1950s and 1960s, everyone in Kotzebue knew all their neighbors. There were not very many houses. The hospital was the largest building. Kotzebue did not have a snowplow to clear the roads. The snow would just pile up, and we could slide wherever we wanted. Where the Alaska Technical Center is now located was all tundra, where we would go and pick berries. Today, if we want to pick berries, we need to go back farther into the hills.

On November 9, 1995, my husband and I celebrated our seventeenth wedding anniversary. Together we have raised four beautiful daughters, two of whom are schooling in the village of Buckland, southwest of Kotzebue. Tina, the oldest, graduated from high school in 1995. Lisa, the next oldest, graduated in 1996.

Also, I'm a grandmother now. Some women can't bear the thought of being grandmothers, but this is life. We can't stop the process of getting older. I love my grandchildren.

Writer Grows Up Eskimo in "Ancient" Alaska

Lucy Nuqarrluk Daniels   Yup'ik   Elim

·Elim

I was born in the fall of 1946 in a small Yup'ik Eskimo village in southeast Alaska. I grew up in a time that now seems like ancient Alaska. In the left back corner of our one-room frame house sat a double-sized bed, commercially made, where Mom, Dad, my little sister, and I slept. My spot was right next to the wall by my sister, who slept next to Mom, who slept next to Dad.

Grandma, Dad's mother, slept in a twin bed—a network of wires on a metal frame—in the right back corner. Grandpa, Mom's father, slept in a wooden twin-sized bed in the right front corner. The wood stove took up the remaining corner.

My older brother, the oldest of us children, I don't remember where he slept. I do remember his treating me like a nuisance, probably because I was four years younger. He and our cousin, a boy his age, used to tease me, laughing as I whined, until my exasperated mother silenced them.

When another sister arrived, I moved to Grandma's bed. Bedtime came when Dad lighted the kerosene lamp and turned off the hissing Coleman lantern or when the generator owner shut off the generator at ten o'clock.

This, of course, was in wintertime. Lying next to Grandma in the soft light, I heard the spooky sound of the earth cracking as it lay frozen. I forgot about the spooks, though, when Grandma began my favorite story.

Her voice barely above a whisper, Grandma spoke, "Once an old woman sat sewing by the light of the window, when a little mouse scampered across the window." (Most likely, the single window was made of seal gut, atop a dome-shaped mudhouse.)

"'Ikaaaaaves-kaves-kaves-kaves-kaves' (Acrooooooss-across-across-across) sang the mouse as it ran. Back and forth the little mouse ran, singing its song, until the old woman became annoyed. Taking her little wooden ladle, she swatted at the mouse and killed it. Saddened by what she had done, the old woman fetched the mouse. She hanged it by its tail and sang to it."

Grandma probably sang the old woman's mourning song, but I don't remember it. Grandpa told stories, too. My brother and our cousin used to sit cross-legged on Grandpa's bed as Grandpa held them spellbound with tales of war and adventure. I only heard snatches of the tales as I went about my own child's play.

Every spring, Grandpa dug flowing ditches to drain mud puddles. I floated many a wood chip down those ditches. A janitor and bell-ringer at the Russian Orthodox Church, Grandpa would come in, probably after lighting the church's oil stove. "Natmum sass'aq ellirta?" [literally, "At where is the clock?" or, "What time is it?"], he asked Mom. Soon after he left, I heard the dong, dong dong—the sound that distinguished the Russian Orthodox Church from the Moravian Church, whose bell went "diling-dalung."

Springtime meant melting snow, Grandpa's drainage ditches, and spring camp. Every April, Mom and Dad pulled my brother and me out of school and took the family to spring camp. Nestled among our belongings in the sled, we took a leisurely dog-team ride to camp.

From our camp we heard the sounds of waterfowl all around us. I especially remember the eerie crying of the loon. Mom and Grandma cut and dried pike and skinned countless muskrat. I helped string the slimy, slithery blackfish onto willow branches to prepare for drying.

Grandma took me along when she went to check the fish net or went egg hunting. I can still hear the swish, swish, swish of the paddle as Grandma guided the canoe over placid waters.

Looking for eggs at an egg-hunting site, I trudged behind Grandma over the spongy tundra. When a mother bird fluttered away ahead of us, we found its eggs right away. When it circled around and around above us, Grandma instructed me to lie down on the ground beside her. When the bird had landed, we walked to where it lay roosting. When we found the nest, Grandma put the eggs into a moss-lined pail, removed the lining of the nest, spit on it, and placed it beside the nest. I still don't know why.

At camp, Grandpa's homemade bow and arrows kept me entertained. Patiently, Grandpa whittled a replacement for each lost arrow. In wintertime, he made me a wooden or moose-horn "storyknife." In the snow that drifted into the porch, my friend and I told each other stories. We flattened and smoothed over a place on the snow (or mud in the summertime) with the storyknife to roughly the size of an 8" x 11" sheet of paper. We drew symbols of the various parts of the story as we talked.

Today's housing projects have made our one-room house a part of a pleasant childhood memory. A network of boardwalks in my home village has rendered Grandpa's drainage ditches quite unnecessary. Commercial chicken eggs, tasteless by comparison, have replaced wild bird eggs. Grandma died and took her stories with her. Spring camps are a thing of the past. BB guns have antiquated Grandpa's bows and arrows. TV, the VCR, and "Super Mario" have become more interesting than "storyknifing."

2

Rural Alaska Life

*I just remind my young generation to be faithful to their great
grandfathers, how they used to live long before we were born,
long before me.* — CHIEF ANDREW ISAAC, Athabascan

In contrast to Alaskans who live in the state's urban centers such as
Anchorage, Fairbanks, and Juneau, where residents typically drive
cars, shop in shopping centers, and lead lives strikingly similar to
residents in other American cities, rural Alaskans live in communities scattered across hundreds of thousands of square miles of territory, not connected by road, remarkably, to the rest of the state.
Rural Alaskans travel by dog team, by motorized four-wheelers, by
boat, by snowmobiles, by aircraft, on foot, and sometimes, within
villages, by car or truck.

In this part of the book, writers offer insight into the difficulties
of rural life as well as the beauty and attraction of living in communities where people maintain close ties to one another.

Although spiritual and linguistic changes have swept into arctic
Alaska at a bewildering rate over the past half-century, the cultural
ways of hunting, fishing, gathering, preparing, and storing foods
remain strong among Native people. Examples are Linda Akeya's
instructions on how to skin a polar bear, Helena Hildreth's revival
of her mother's jam-making tradition, and Hannah Paniyavluk
Loon's directions on how to harvest *masru*, or wild Eskimo
potatoes, by searching the nests of field mice. Hannah's daughter,
Shona Greist Andrews, shares knowledge about an edible wild
plant, sourdock. A hungry John Cleveland offers a graphic descrip-
tion of how he devoured a muskrat out on the trail, and Spencer
Rearden shows appreciation for the particular challenges of trapping a fox and for his father who taught him how. Carol Harris explains the fine art of making seal oil, a traditional delicacy of
coastal Eskimos.

Julia Stalker tells of sharing Native foods and their symbolic role
in ceremonies and family rituals. Sandy Russell explains the experi-

ence of a traditional blanket toss, part of her healing process and rehabilitation at the Anvil Mountain Correctional Center in Nome that includes engaging in cultural activities. With no trees, Kotzebue residents mostly burn expensive fuel oil in their homes, although an illustrious resident such as Jimmie Evak describes how to save money by collecting shipping pallets around town and cutting them up to feed a wood stove.

Rural lifestyles typically mix subsistence with jobs tied to the cash economy. Genny Norris of Shungnak in Northwest Alaska characterizes the subsistence way of life so vital to her community. Dolly Arnold explains how traditional Iñupiaq values fit in with operating a contemporary family business. Boyuck Ryan's harrowing story tells about commercial fishing as a way to earn a living.

Finally, a short anecdote best sums up the idiom of life in rural Alaska. Once a student left a message for his professor explaining why he wouldn't be able to make it to English class that evening: "Gramps got a whale in Barrow," the note said, meaning that his first responsibility was to family and community to help haul the whale onto land and carve up the meat and blubber to share with Barrow's extended family.

Native Food Nourishes the Body and More

Julia Jones Anausuk Stalker   Iñupiaq   Kotzebue

I am originally from Selawik, which is where I grew up in the 1960s. I recall the days in Selawik when we had only Native food to eat. It is called niqipiaq, meaning food prepared off the land. In those days store-bought foods were so scarce, we ate niqipiaq almost everyday. Today, we still enjoy those foods and sharing the delicious meals and the company of others and indulging in our favorite foods that are set on the table.

Niqipiaq is served for many occasions including family gatherings such as birthdays, holidays, or a welcoming party for visiting family. At such events the table will be filled with a variety of niqipiaq. You have a choice of which food you want to eat, such as dried caribou meat and dried fish: white, pike, or salmon. Frozen white fish, or trout (quaq), is laid on the table to thaw just enough to easily cut. Seal oil is also placed on the table.

Vegetables that are rendered in seal oil spice up one's plate. These vegetables include a certain kind of leaves called sura and wild celery, which is rare today. Berries for dessert also are placed on the table, which is the best part of the meal for a satisfied stomach. Salmonberries (aqpiks), blackberries, and blueberries are mixed in a bowl and usually served plain or as Eskimo ice cream.*

*Eskimo ice cream usually is made of a combination of fat, sweetener, and berries, for instance whipped Crisco or seal oil, sugar, and blueberries. Fish may also be added.

Besides taking pleasure in the eating, we are taught to hunt the right kind of animal or pick the right plants and to prepare these foods at the right time. A book about this called Plants That We Eat, written by Anore Jones, was dedicated to the "Old-time Eskimo people, Utuqqanaat Iñupiat" and to "The young Eskimo people, Nutaat Iñupiat." It shows where and what to pick in the summer. The dedication adds a message to the Iñupiat: "That they may learn and use it, blending the best with other culture . . . and that they may pass it on."

Gathering and storing of food have changed greatly. In the days of my late grandfather, life was hard. To hunt, the Iñupiat went on foot, by qayaq (canoe), or with dog teams. They did not have snowmachines to rely on, nor did they have freezers to save their food. According to Elmer Imgusriq Ballot, an Elder who told a story in the lore of the Iñupiat entitled "Ways That Are No More," "We did not enjoy any frozen food during the summer as people do now."

Native food also fills a hunter's grub box. My dad was a great hunter as I recall. He knew when and where to go for all the different food. For survival, he took along a grub box full of niqipiaq in case he got trapped in bad weather. My mom in the same manner went out to pick greens and fruits off the land.

The foods we eat also connect us with the experience of going out in the country. Our energy comes from the land we live on. Our health and happiness are restored by our daily diet. Niqipiaq has all the vitamins and minerals that our bodies require. A similar philosophy is expressed by people of another culture: authors Michio and Aveline Kushi who wrote *Macrobiotic Dietary Recommendations*, stating that "food is our source of being" and that "to eat is to take in the whole environment." We all have such a way to connect our lives to the earth.

Today, we are encouraged to continue this essential part of our Iñupiaq heritage. For our children and their children, we know how important it is to feed from our land while we still can. Our foods define who we are, connect us to the land and keep our culture alive.

How to Skin a Polar Bear

Savoonga

Linda Akeya   *Siberian Yup'ik*   *Savoonga*

Polar bears are among the biggest and most powerful animals on earth. They have strong hind legs, which makes them fast runners, but they also can use their front legs to catch and kill a human being or other animals, such as seals, walrus, and fish.

I had no experience in butchering a polar bear; therefore, I asked one of my uncles about it. He invited me to watch him and the men

in my village skin a bear, because they are the ones who know best.

Cutting a polar bear is very easy, just like saying the alphabet or counting ones, twos, threes, and so on.

To start, turn the body over so that the bear is lying on its back. Then cut from the belly-button all the way to the chin and continue across the arms from one end to the other in the shape of a cross.

From the belly, cut to the bottom of the body and to the legs. The easy part is now over, but the hard part comes in butchering the hands and the feet.

First separate the nails from the joints of the hands and the feet. It is a tough thing to do, so do not rush. If you don't know how to separate the joints, ask someone who does to help you.

Once the front is finished, remove the skin from the meat; it is like peeling the skin from an apple.

Cutting the back part of the body is a lot quicker than the front. It takes only a few minutes to skin the back, but you still need to be very careful not to make holes in the skin. If you do make a hole, you can sew it up later, when the skin is completely dried.

At this point, the head should still be attached to the skin. Just like cutting the feet and the hands, you need to take some time on the head. For the last step, the meat is separated from the bones and the guts are thrown away.

The skin is then washed at the beach and hung to dry at a food-storage shelter or outside the house of the person who killed the polar bear. Our culture says that whoever sees the polar bear first on land gets to keep the skin. But on the ocean, the boat captain gets to keep the skin even if one of his crew members may have seen it first. The captain gives out the meat to whomever would like it. This tradition has been going on for many generations.

Some people can't stand eating the meat, and I am one of these people, but the fur I wouldn't mind keeping.

The polar bear's white-yellowish fur is long and thick. It is beautiful and can be made into different things, for instance, a jacket, mittens, hat, ruff [the collar around the head opening on a parka], mukluks, or even Eskimo yo-yos.

Kotzebue

Making Jam from Fresh Tundra Berries Recalls Memories

Helena Hildreth   Iñupiaq-Yup'ik   *Kotzebue*

When I was growing up on the windswept coast of western Alaska, every summer it was a tradition in our family to help our parents pick enough berries to last us the winter. My dad gave us a choice: pick berries or stay home, clean up, and have dinner made by the time the berry pickers came home. I always opted to go out for the day and pick berries.

My mom used a homemade wooden comb to pick blueberries, and we sometimes used our homemade wooden buckets with ivory handles, although we preferred to use plastic buckets instead because they could hold more. I liked to pick berries where they were abundant because it was easier and faster.

Mom would always take some dried fish and seal oil, which we ate for lunch on the tundra, with the sun shining and the wind blowing in our faces. Of course, we would never go berry picking if it was raining or if no breeze was keeping the bugs away.

My mom always stocked our pantry with homemade jam made

Iñupiaq-Yup'ik Helena
Hildreth. Kotzebue,
Alaska, 1992. Photo
by Jim Magdanz.

from the berries we picked. Now that I'm on my own, I enjoy picking berries each summer, either to eat fresh for dessert or to make
jams to put aside for the winter months.

I learned how to make jam from blueberries, salmonberries, or
any kind of berries a couple of years ago. I followed directions from
a recipe on a box of fruit pectin I bought at the store. I figured that
the only way I was ever going to learn how to make jam was to try it

Historical subsistence from the land: Iñupiaq boy in Shungnak, Alaska, an inland village some 150 miles east of Kotzebue. Cranberries, blueberries, and salmonberries, a traditional subsistence food, are all found in abundance in northwestern Alaska. John M. Brooks Photograph Collection, accession number UA68-32-141N, in the Elmer E. Rasmuson Library Archives, Alaska and Polar Regions Department, University of Alaska Fairbanks.

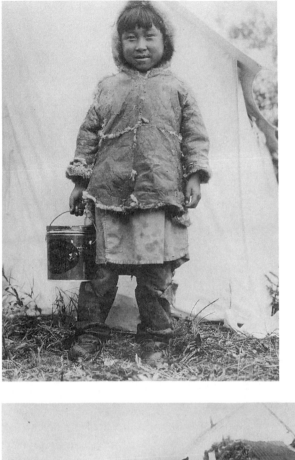

Historical subsistence from the land: Eskimo berry pickers in Nome, Alaska, circa 1925. More than ten species of wild fruit grow in Alaska, including the especially abundant lowbush cranberry and blueberry. Albert J. Johnson Photograph Collection, accession number 89-166-401N, in the Elmer E. Rasmuson Library Archives, Alaska and Polar Regions Department, University of Alaska Fairbanks.

myself, regardless of whether it turned out to be a flop. I didn't have family around to show me how this time.

I have had to learn from my mistakes—for instance, in ladling the jam into jars. I am careful not to rush this process now, because at this stage, the jam is very hot, because it has been boiling. A few times, I almost sent a jar of hot liquids crashing to the floor because of being burned by these hot jars. Now I use a sturdy potholder to prevent such mishaps.

This process takes about an hour, and by the evening, I can tell if my jam has turned out successfully because it should be in a jell form by then. It takes a lot of muster to plan this process and actually do it, but I have found that if I believe in what I'm doing and have confidence through it all, everything will turn out right.

Fox Snaring, a Painstaking Art

.Kotzebue

Spencer Rearden   *Yup'ik*   *Kotzebue*

When I was young, I used to tag along with my dad to check his fox snares. By observing, I learned the tricks he used to catch fox. Now that I'm older, I go out every year on our snowmachine to set snares.

From early December to late February is a good time to snare fox. At that time of year, their fur gleams in prime condition, with long, red guard hairs. Guard hairs are the outermost and longest hairs that make the fur glimmer.

Fox snaring can be tricky. Their keen sense of smell makes them very cautious and difficult to outsmart. I prepare to catch fox by making snares out of airplane cable and a washer. Then I wash the snares, wax them, and use clean gloves with no scent, to store them in plastic bags.

It would seem that the best place to catch a fox would be at its den. The abundance of tracks and the small entrance hole make it look easy. But the cautious fox usually won't go into its den after snares are set. Setting snares on a snowmachine trail usually works better. The foxes prefer to travel on the hard-packed snow rather than on the deep, soft snow. I usually look for a place where a fox would least expect a problem, such as in willows or in tall grass.

Iñupiaq John Cleveland.
Selawik, Alaska, 1992.
Photo by Jim Magdanz.

The anticipation and the thrill of catching a fox keeps me awake in bed at night sometimes. I wonder if a fox is in or about to enter my snare. I worry if I did something wrong. Did I leave my tracks or a scent that would scare the fox?

When the day comes for me to check the snares, I race to see if I got anything. Sometimes I get lucky and catch a beautiful red fox. Or, maybe it's not luck: The credit for what I've learned in order to catch a fox goes to my dad.

•Selawik

Quick Meal of Muskrat Serves As Nourishment on the Trail

John Cleveland   Iñupiaq   Selawik

Once when I went hunting with a kayak, I took no snack and did not eat before I left the village. I had planned on staying out only a few hours, but somehow those hours turned into a challenging day and night. I was too far away to paddle back home for dinner, so scraping together a quick meal was imperative. A muskrat, which I was lucky enough to have caught, would be my only source of food. I landed my kayak, built a fire, and started to skin the animal.

I first cut off the forepaws, then moved to the hind legs, cutting around the legs where it meets the paws. I separated the fur from the paws. Then I cut up from the paws toward the tail on both sides and around the tail. I then started skinning the fur off the flesh, starting from the back, working my way around to the belly. The legs were easy to skin, but I had to be careful, as always, skinning around the testicles. I had to make sure I didn't cut into a testicle, for this would have created a foul smell, making it hard for me to continue skinning the muskrat.

When one is hungry enough, the skin can be pulled up toward the head, while holding the legs and tail with the other hand, and I was hungry enough that day. After I stripped the fur up to the neck, I started using a knife again for the head.

I then removed the fur from the body and cut a two-inch slash on the skin over the ribs big enough to slide two fingers underneath. I used my fingers to help guide the blade tip down toward the tail without cutting the intestines. I knew the intestines also would smell if I cut them. I then got the intestines to fall out when the animal was turned back on its belly. Instead of cutting up the ribs, I worked underneath them to pull out the throat, lungs, and heart. I cut off the head to help in taking the throat out.

When all that was done, I took the muskrat down to the water and washed off the excessive blood. My next step was to cut down a straight willow. I then built up the fire again, cut the muskrat's tail off and stuffed it into the chest cavity, then skewered the animal with the willow. As I held the muskrat over the fire, I started drooling from the pleasant aroma of the roasting meat.

I held the stick in my hand, turning and turning the muskrat. When it began to look leathery-brown, I took it off the fire and started feasting. I was so hungry that I ate the spine after clearing away the ribs. The spine was very crunchy.

Iñupiaq Woman Learns How to Search for Mouse Caches

Hannah Paniyavluk Loon   Iñupiaq   Kotzebue

I dedicate this piece to Vera Douglas, Larry Custer, and Rosie and Elmer Ward, who live in the villages of Shungnak and Kobuk in Northwest Alaska, to remember the day we spent searching for nivi, or mouse caches, in fall 1989. We shared many laughs, good food, tea, and teamwork while out fishing and gathering roots. I offer this piece with taikuułallak, or many thanks, to my friends on the Upper Kobuk River in Northwest Alaska for being patient teachers and good company.

Kuuvanmiut, which means "Kobuk River people" in Iñupiaq enjoy searching for nivi, or mouse caches, which are filled with a variety of roots, each fall—a busy period for most people of the Northwest Arctic region of Alaska.

During this season, caribou migrate across the river, giving men the opportunity to go hunting for their winter meat supply. Meanwhile, the women travel farther upriver to their camps to fish for salmon and sheefish. Then, after the strenuous tasks of hunting and fishing, Kuuvanmiut leisurely spend the last few days at camp watching the fall colors change, the birds in flight, and the moose as they roam about, as well as cooking on an open fire and boating upriver to nivinniaq, or "search for mouse caches." Nivinniaq rewards Kuuvanmiut after the hard work of daily living.

Also in the fall, the mouse population has been busy digging into the ground for masru, also called wild Eskimo potatoes, which are brown-stemmed and medium-sized in appearance—the rodent's main diet. The mice inhabit what is called an iglu, which consists of a home for them plus an average of from three to four init (rooms) where roots are stored.

When the first frost comes, it is time for the people to search for roots. Rather than gathering roots one by one as the mice do,

Upper Kobuk, a region of Alaska known for its scenic beauty. The Kobuk River, Alaska's ninth largest, runs roughly parallel to the Arctic Circle—north of it—for 347 miles. Photo by John Creed.

Kuuvanmiut harvest large quantities of masru from mouse caches. Kuuvanmiut search for nivi around mid-September, before the ground freezes solid.

Let me explain how to find masru. Because this activity requires hiking through wooded areas, you should carry tools needed for protection and for gathering masru. A pickax, called a *siklaq*, for digging is commonly used, or a hammer may be substituted. Also, you need a straight, narrow stick to probe the ground for soft, hollow spots. Always take along a high-powered rifle in case of bear, as well as a pack filled with snacks, old dried fish or meat, plastic bags, tissues, matches, old gloves, and water or some other kind of beverage.

If a partner accompanies you, he or she looks for other iglu in the same area. Always remember to build a small fire to make bears aware of your presence, especially when you have walked a long distance.

Nivi can be found anywhere you see signs of mouse activity along the islands and beaches of the Kobuk River. For instance, look for mounds of dirt and little trails left by the mice. Certain people have a good eye for nivi, and some do not. But do not worry: If you are not good at discovering mounds of caches, the other *nivinniaqtuat* (those searching for nivi) will share their masru with you.

When you find a mound, simply probe it with your stick or gently step on the ground to see if it is soft. Open the soft spot with the pick and lift the top layer out gently. Using a pair of old gloves, feel around in the hollow area for roots.

Some people feel squeamish about reaching into a cache for fear of accidentally grabbing hold of a mouse. So take the mouse off your mind and be thankful for the rodent's hard work, which enables you to harvest masru from its nivi.

When you find a nivi filled from one to two inches deep with brown roots that have white centers, bingo! you have struck the side dish for your dinner.

Some people greedily take all the masru, but conservative persons spread the roots out on a piece of plastic and select only the large pieces for themselves. Then they return smaller pieces and other roots back to the chamber. A small piece of *paniqtuq* (dried fish) is placed in the chamber as repayment for the mouse's hard work. This expresses thanks according to Kuuvanmiut's customary values.

Finally, to repair the nivi, break up small twigs around you and use them as a foundation to replace the ground you lifted out earlier. If grasses are available, place them over the sticks and cover the iglu.

You can find good-quality and sweeter masru if you wait until after the ground frosts over. Try breaking one root in half. If it snaps crisply, then you have found good masru. Searching for masru is something like Julia Child selecting quality mushrooms for her gourmet cooking.

Masru are washed and preserved in oil, and they taste sweet when accompanied with bear fat or seal oil. A nourishing food, they are not served in large amounts but as a side dish with dried or frozen fish.

While the idea behind looking for nivi is to gather food, searching for them also is relaxing for the mind, body, and soul. It gets you away from home for a while to enjoy the last days of fall before winter comes.

Iñupiaq Recipe for Cooking
and Gathering Sourdock

Shona Greist Nasruluk Andrews   Iñupiaq   Kotzebue

Sourdock has been gathered and stored for centuries by Natives in the Arctic region of Alaska. Quaġaq, which means sourdock in the Iñupiaq language, is a green edible plant that grows on the tundra and is just as nutritious and tasty to Iñupiaq gatherers as cabbage is to people in the Lower 48 states. There are many ways to cook quaġaq, but the benefits are astounding to a niqipiaq (Native food) lover in Northwest Alaska. When handled so as to preserve the ascorbic acid, these plants can take the place of hard-to-get oranges and tomatoes, the dependable ascorbic acid foods in our usual diets, according to a Cooperative Extension Service publication of the University of Alaska. Quaġaq apparently has played a major role in our Native people's traditional diets that have sustained us for many generations.

Ruminex arcticus is the Latin name for sourdock, which is also known as "arctic dock" or "wild spinach." "Quaġaq is highly prized by the Eskimos," say Cooperative Extension Service officials. In Webster's New World Dictionary, I didn't find the two words sour and dock together. I looked up the word "sour," though, which means "having a sharp acid taste, as in vinegar." "Dock" means "to cut off the end." To eat sourdock, we cut up the leaves, which are somewhat sour.

Before you think you can cut sourdocks and cook them, make sure to look for them on a nice, windy day while the sky is bright. While you enjoy the fresh air, walk slowly and gaze at the tundra. Observe if there are any six-inch to four-foot-high, red, cone-shaped flowers, indicating sourdock.

The quaġaq is formed by a single stem that is stiff. It is reddish violet at the base of the flowers. The flowers on the top half of the plants are small and either completely green or green tinged with

Historical subsistence from the land: Besides providing food, tundra plants are used for medicinal teas and healing substances. Alaskan Shepherd Photo Collection, accession number 88-117-228N, in the Elmer E. Rasmuson Library Archives, Alaska and Polar Regions Department, University of Alaska Fairbanks.

purple. Alongside them are seed pods, which are red capsules.

Sourdocks don't look as if they have leaves when seen in the grasses, because the leaves grow at the base. These smooth leaves are green and can grow up to ten inches long, according to the book, *The Plants That We Eat.*

Sourdock grows in wet places and along brackish marshes. In the Selawik area, we have found them on the sides of the rivers. Many of my relatives prefer to gather quaġaq with trash bags because they are lighter and easier to handle than other containers.

You can pick these leaves all summer long, but mid-July is the preferred time to pick them, when they are plentiful. Until the frost withers them, the leaves are edible. People pick sourdock with or without stems. Either way, I guarantee that this delicious plant satisfies our stomachs. You can do many things with quaġaq, but a meal made in our family every summer is the "half-cooked sourdock." To cook *Rumex arcticus,* cut them in half and boil them from three to ten minutes. After they are cooked much like spinach, drain the water. Now they are ready to freeze.

How to Make Seal Oil

Carol Harris   Iñupiaq   Kotzebue

During the summer, my family and I go to our summer camp in Sisualik, located about thirteen miles across the sound from Kotzebue in Northwest Alaska, to gather our winter food supply. One of the many traditional activities we pursue there is making dried seal meat and seal oil.

Each spring my stepfather, Raymond, and my brothers, Jimmy, Ray, and Calvin, go hunting in the Chukchi Sea for bearded seals or ugruks, as we Iñupiat call them. The hunters catch the ugruks and put them on the ice, where they cut the stomach just enough to take the guts out. Next, they put the guts into plastic bags to use for dog food. Then they put the intestines, kidneys, liver and heart back into the ugruk.

While Raymond and the boys are out hunting, Mom and I prepare our cutting place either by using plywood boards or by flattening big boxes and spreading them out on the ground. This keeps the meat and blubber clean. When the hunters return home, they pull the ugruks over to our cutting areas.

To prepare an ugruk, first take out the intestines, kidneys, liver and heart to cook later. Now cut from the stomach to the neck, then around the neck. Next, cut from the stomach to the flippers, then go around the flippers to just above the tail. After that, cut around the fin and bend the fin down to locate the joint. Cut through the joint on each fin.

Next, separate the blubber from the meat until all the blubber falls off the carcass. Put the blubber aside to sit for a day or two.

Now you are ready to start butchering the ugruk meat. First, remove the brisket bone from the front of the ribs. Next, cut the meat from the side of the ugruk, and cut as close as possible to the bone all the way to the backbone. After that, cut the ribs off the backbone by cutting through the joints. Remove the backbone from the pelvic bone by cutting through the joint. Then split the ham bone and cut a hole through the ham meat. Hang it on a drying rack for two to three days, depending on the weather.

After hanging the meat on the drying rack for at least a day or two, cut the meat into strips and let them dry for about four to five days, depending, again, on the weather. After the meat dries, cut it into three- to four-inch strips. Put the meat into boxes until the oil is ready.

To prepare the blubber, first cut it away from the skin in blocks. Then cut the blubber into thin strips and put them in wooden barrels or five-gallon buckets.

After cutting the blubber, put it in "cold storage," which for us is a hole in the ground about three feet deep, six feet long, and six feet wide. The top is built like an A-frame house, which is covered with moss and sod from the tundra.

Check the blubber every day to see if it is ready to add the dried meat. When the blubber is all melted, it has become what is called "seal oil," and it is ready for the meat to be added.

In the fall, we move our fresh seal oil to Kotzebue, where we put it in our freezer to enjoy all winter.

·Kotzebue

Using Pallets to Warm Your Home

Jimmie Evak   Iñupiaq   Kotzebue

This winter, I am using wood as a primary source of heat in my home in Kotzebue, even though no trees grow in this Arctic coast community I call home.

I use two kinds of wood: logs and pallets. Each spring, I get logs from the ocean beach after the rivers break up and carry them down to coastal Kotzebue. Unfortunately, this supply is limited because other people in Kotzebue have the same idea, so I gather what I can and supplement logs with wooden pallets from various businesses around town.

From my experience, I would like to offer some pointers on using pallets to heat your home in Kotzebue.

Of course, in order to burn pallets, you must have a wood stove. Be sure to choose a wood stove that can handle twenty-inch or longer logs. It also should be a heavy, cast-iron stove. Make sure to

Iñupiaq Jimmie Evak.
Kotzebue, Alaska,
1992. Photo by Jim
Magdanz.

hook up the stove correctly. Use the right parts, such as metalbestos pipes, which run up through your roof and ceiling. Also, use heat shields around the stove to prevent fires. For further safety, especially for sleeping, install a smoke detector.

Pallets are abundant in Kotzebue because so many goods are shipped here on pallets. Stores and other organizations are usually happy that someone will haul them away, but always ask an employee at the site of a local business first, to see it if is okay to do so.

Think ahead. During the summer and early fall, most people will not be worried about pallets because it is still so warm out. When it starts to get cold, however, the "stampede" starts. Start gathering pallets when it is warm out, for it will save you many cold trips in sub-zero weather.

Pile your pallets fifteen to twenty high, and neatly, so that when the snow comes, they will still be easy to find. Use either a chain saw or electric saw to cut your pallets. If you use an electric saw, use carbide-tipped blades, which are more expensive but do keep their edge longer.

Have a place picked out to pile your wood inside the house at a safe distance from the stove. A plywood box keeps the wood stacked neatly and also keeps the sharp edges and nails away from young children. You might also provide a space in the storm shed or outside the house near the door to pile with wood, so that in extremely cold or stormy weather, you do not have to work outside. If you stack your cut pallets outside, build a rack with the bottom raised a few feet above the ground to keep the cut firewood from getting covered with snow.

Inside the house, keep some cardboard stored inside a box so your fire starting will go easier each morning. Also, keep some wood cut into kindling to help start a fire. Use a hatchet or big knife to cut kindling.

When burning pallets, creosote will build up in the chimney. That means regular cleaning of your chimney is necessary. Buy a can of chimney cleaner powder or sticks, or a chimney brush to clean your pipes. If you do not clean your pipes, you will be sorry when you have to move into the local homeless shelter.

Because nails also pose a problem with pallets, keep a few coffee cans, thick leather gloves, and a small wood-stove shovel handy so that you can remove those pallet nails once in a while. Transfer the hot ashes and nails into the coffee cans, which should then be put in the snow to cool them off faster. Then toss the contents into a cardboard box and haul them out to the dump yourself, because the city garbage collectors will not pick them up.

Using pallets does have some disadvantages. It takes time and effort to haul, cut, and stack the pallets. You also have to clean your stove frequently of nails. I prefer logs to pallets, but necessity has always been the mother of invention, and I do keep my home and family warm with pallets all winter.

•Shungnak

Subsistence Means Keeping Busy Year-Round

Genevieve Norris   Iñupiaq   Shungnak

In many rural communities, the people rely on subsistence hunting and fishing for their livelihood. The word subsistence means "the manner of keeping alive." Subsistence is a way of obtaining food and shelter—the necessities of life. Subsisting is the condition of remaining alive.

For the people in my community, subsistence remains very pertinent to our culture. Jobs are limited in small villages like Shungnak,

Shungnak, Alaska. Two boys returning home from rabbit hunting on a midwinter day. Shungnak, an upriver village of 237 residents, lies 150 miles east of Kotzebue. 1980. Photo by Jim Magdanz.

so many of the people depend on subsistence in order to provide food and clothing for their families. I know of two families in my area who subsist and live year-round, away from the village, at camp.

Some people pursue subsistence food gathering primarily during the summer months. Hunting and fishing provide food and clothing. Take caribou hunting, for instance. The meat is prepared for food and can be cut up to dry or put away to freeze. The skin is used to make clothing such as parkas, mittens, and mukluks.

There are other useful purposes for the caribou hide. I have seen my mother prepare a whole caribou hide to make leather rope. To do this, first she saturates the hide with soapy water, folds it up, then places it in a bag or box. Then she leaves it to soak this way for at least a week. Soaking causes the hair to be removed easily from the caribou hide. My mother then washes and strips the hide with a sharp knife, making strips as thin as spaghetti. When this thin leathery rope is dry, my father can use it to make snowshoes and basket sleds.

Fishing is another means of gathering food. Fish can be dried and smoked in preparation for winter use. The people here in our area catch salmon and white fish more abundantly than any other kinds of fish. Fish provides food for both the people and the dogs.

The women can pick blueberries, salmonberries, cranberries, and blackberries during the summer and store them away for winter. Virtually any kind of berry can be made into jelly or jam.

Edible greens such as wild spinach and rhubarb also are picked by the people for subsistence use. These usually are cooked before they are stored. A wooden barrel is used for storage, especially for berries and the greens.

These are just a few examples of how I, as a Native resident living in a rural village, have practiced and have seen my people live a subsistence life. Since Mother Nature supplies mostly everything we need, subsistence is a matter of knowing how and when to hunt, fish, and gather. To me, subsistence is a way of supporting life.

Sisters Incorporate Traditional Values in Modern Business

Dolly Arnold   *Iñupiaq*   *Kotzebue*

·Kotzebue

On a winter day on March 15, 1965, I was the sixth child born to my mother, Dorothy, and my late father, Clarence Arnold Sr. Although I was raised in Kotzebue, located thirty miles above the Arctic Circle in Northwest Alaska, I was born in Noorvik, located about forty-five miles northeast of Kotzebue. My six sisters, Aggie, Sarah, Wanda, Mona, Francis, and Valarie, my brother, Clarence Jr., and I all grew up with a strong sense of our traditional Iñupiaq values that today help support a successful family business.

With having such a big family to support, my dad was an avid subsistence hunter and fisher who provided, in abundance, caribou, moose, and fish for my siblings and me. I remember from the tender age of four years how my older sisters and my mom would all share the responsibilities of skinning and butchering the caribou and moose. I distinctly recall my dad telling everyone that we must learn never to waste any part of an animal. With the knowledge my dad acquired from the Elders while growing up, he taught us ways to make use of the entire animal, such as using the caribou skin for making mukluks or saving the whole pelt that he and other hunters

Iñupiaq Valarie Romane (nee Arnold), sister of writer Dolly Arnold and partner in the fur-hat family business. Kotzebue, Alaska, 1992. Photo by Jim Magdanz.

used to lie on at night while out scoping the mountains and valleys for caribou or moose.

Consequently, we learned the traditional Iñupiaq value — respect for nature — a long time ago, and today I believe this Iñupiaq value and the value of hard work are embodied in "Sarah's Hat Works," a business created in 1985 by my sister, Sarah, along with help from another sister, Valarie, and me.

Sarah launched her business during a sluggish time in Alaska's construction trade, from which her husband Marc used to earn a living for his entire family. Sarah believed she could make extra money to help pay the bills, including buying groceries for a family of seven, by making and selling traditional fur hats.

My sister began Sarah's Hat Works by taking a trapper-style fur hat worn throughout Alaska and adapting her own pattern to it. Today, Sarah's fur hats consist of different types of fur such as beaver, fox, and rabbit fashioned into a traditional Iñupiaq style. The traditional Iñupiaq hat is made out of fur on the inside flaps and on the outside front panel, as well as man-made material that makes up the lining. A full fur hat, on the other hand, is made entirely out of fur that shows on the outside. We also make a hat that is called a "pill box" for women and that has no ear flaps.

In keeping with the Iñupiaq's traditional respect for nature, we have learned not to waste any part of a pelt. We always use a majority of the pelt for the fur hats. What's left of the pelt, such as material surrounding the perimeter of the traced hat pattern, we use for a variety of arts and crafts. For example, the soft belly part of a beaver we use to make cuffs that are sewn onto the end of a parka sleeve. We also make ear muffs, depending on the type of fur we use, and key chain trinkets and whatever else our imaginative minds can think of.

My sisters and I had not sewn fur skins for a long time before Sarah's Hat Works began, so at first we had to learn from our mistakes. I remember sewing two parts of a fur hat that did not belong together, and the hat came out lop-sided as if I were making some sort of concoction for Halloween. I'll never forget when my sister Valarie made her first full fur hat, because she sewed it inside out! The skin side was on the outside when it was supposed to be on the inside.

The most memorable time we have had of working diligently to fill demands was before Fur Rondy, a festival held in Anchorage each February. Our goal was to sew as many fur hats as possible to make enough money for rent, food, and utility bills. We made two hundred hats!

When I think about this, my hands want to get stiff because of the intricate sewing that has to be done to make a perfect hat. If we made mistakes, we could not throw the piece away because we did not want to waste materials. We had to tear the hat apart and begin all over again. Such work takes patience, a comfortable chair, and a sharp needle. Precise stitches are important because a customer's satisfaction is always our ultimate goal.

Throughout the tenure of Sarah's Hat Works, we all have had to work together closely to make a quality finished product. For example, my mother, Dorothy, has made the yarn strings, my sister Valarie has put together the fur balls, my sister Sarah has made the lining and copied her pattern onto the skin side of a pelt, and I have traced the pattern on leather and cut them out. We exchange duties often to keep from getting bored.

Because our family worked with real diligence, Sarah's Hat Works became a successful business. For many long nights, we labored to sew the hats perfectly, and now our work has become known throughout Alaska and even in some of the Lower 48 states.

.Unalakleet

A Boat's-Eye View of Fishing on the Norton Sound

Wilfred "Boyuck" Ryan   Iñupiaq   Unalakleet

In the spring of 1989, I worked the herring fishing season on Norton Sound in Northwest Alaska for the first time from inside a twenty-four-foot aluminum boat—an exhausting, dangerous experience.

Normally during herring season, I sit in the left seat of an airplane, piloting either fish biologists or buyers and fishermen into the area. During this particular season, though, Linda, my sister, was my "pilot" as the boat's captain. Our friend Cal and I were crew members.

We spent many hours preparing for the fishing expedition. We had to wash the boat, fix the hydraulic system and the outboard motors, mend the nets, and pack camping gear for our journey to Golsovia on Norton Sound.

After a two-hour boat ride, we arrived at our destination only to find that our "secluded" camping site had been transformed into a canvas city. More than one hundred people were living in thirty tents on an acre of land.

Out in the harbor, forty herring boats, three processing ships, eight tender boats, and four hundred fishing boats from St. Michael to Shaktoolik were waiting for the fishing period to open.

We listened on the vhf marine radio for the fish biologist to announce the opening, but on the first day, that announcement never came.

Early the next morning, though, the state biologist responsible for regulating the fishing periods announced on the marine radio, "The fishing season will open for four hours today, from noon to 4 p.m."

Hearing this news, Cal, Linda, and I devoured our breakfast, then spread our nets inside the boat. Cal hung anchors on the side of the boat while I coiled the anchor lines to keep them from tangling. Linda packed snacks and drinks in plastic Ziploc bags. We dressed in our fishing gear, which included rubber boots, rain gear, rubber gloves, and sweat bands. We were ready to fish.

Cal drove the boat out of the harbor to the location Linda had selected. When we arrived, I dropped the anchor and guided the anchor line and net onto the bow roller. As we propelled in reverse, the net spread into the water.

"Our net is floating!" Linda said.

I thought this meant that the monofilament mesh we were using was defective. To my surprise, it meant that the net was already full of fish. I threw out the second anchor. We repeated the process. Soon our second net was in the water.

The vast ocean rapidly diminished in size. Aluminum boats crashed into each other and nets thrashed in all directions. People's cursing overshadowed the banging of the hydraulic shakers. Propeller blades whined in the air and motors quit under heavy loads. The smell of outboard exhaust laced the air.

"It's time to pull in—grab the anchor!" Cal shouted.

After securing both cork and anchor line to the hydraulic roller, our hard work started. Every ten feet of net weighed several hundred pounds as we shook the small one-pound fish from it. Fifty minutes later, thousands of fish were flapping about on the bottom of the boat.

The net was clean and we were in the process of resetting. I threw out the anchor. Cal drove backwards while Linda and I held the net on the roller as it fell freely into the water. This cycle of setting, pulling, shaking, and resetting continued until our boat was loaded with fish. That left only four inches of "freeboard," or the space between the lip of the boat and the surface of the water.

We maneuvered our boat toward the tender boat, where five metric tons of fish were sucked through a twelve-inch vacuum line in a matter of minutes. Our first delivery went smoothly, and we returned to the nets for another load.

During the second delivery, though, the wind velocity had increased to about thirty knots, causing five-foot swells in the sea. As we sailed next to the tender boat, a huge wave slammed against us. The outside of our boat rode the wave, but the inside wedged under the lip of the huge vessel. The sea rushed into our boat.

"We're swamping!" I said.

"Shovel the fish to the outside!" Cal commanded.

A gust of wind dislodged us from the larger boat. I shoveled fish while we drifted away at a thirty-degree tilt, still taking on water. Cal maneuvered to dock once more. Just as we reached the tender, our boat started sinking. The tender's crew threw us several lines, but it was too late to worry about mooring.

"Shovel!" Cal shouted.

"Forget the shoveling. Pass me the rope!" I countered. I tied a knot standing knee-deep in water and fish. Cal grabbed the vacuum pump and sucked sea water, fish, and raincoats through the tube. After a few minutes, our boat floated normally again.

Still shaking, I asked Cal to pass me a Coke. Breathless and stricken by the thought of potential tragedy, we leaned into the side of the boat in silence.

Upon returning to our nets, we found them floating and full of fish.

"Man, we only have thirty-five minutes before the period closes!" Linda said.

"Run the roller at full speed. Don't slow it down. Boyuck and I will shake the nets," Cal told her.

The gas engine labored at full throttle, burdened with the heavy load of fish. Linda mumbled something about fish getting stuck in the roller.

"Shake toward the rear! We're getting too heavy up front," Cal shouted.

I thought of the fish warden and the fine he would levy if we were caught with our net in the water at closing time. Sweat flowed in streams down my brow onto my glasses, fogging the lenses until my vision blurred. My leg muscles started to cramp and my fingers froze in a grabbing position, but I kept shaking the nets.

One minute remained until closing time. An airplane cruised overhead. I looked up and noticed the anchor line stretching from the bow roller into the water. The nets were rolled safely in the boat, and we were standing up to our hips in three feet of herring.

On the way to deliver our catch, I removed my rain gear to cool off. I took off my glasses, which were covered with herring scales. Cal's face contorted in the sunlight. Linda's hair was wet and tangled in herring slime. We laughed in unison at the sight of us — wet, ragged, and tired.

We also were hungry and thirsty. Linda found our lunch beneath a foot of herring. I realized then why she had taken the extra precaution in wrapping the sandwiches, crackers, and cookies.

We waited for several hours in line, to take our turn again at the tender's vacuum pump. Cal shoveled and I guided the vacuum line. When tired, we exchanged duties until we had unloaded the last fish. Then we moved to a pressurized water pump to wash the coat of herring scales, slime, and eggs off the boat. Meanwhile, Linda stayed on the tender to oversee the biologist as he measured the percentage of egg maturity, which is the method of determining the buying price.

Once on shore, we prepared a meal of barbecued chicken, roast potatoes, and coffee, which we shared with other campers, who contributed roast ugruk, muktuk, dried fish, dried ugruk meat, seal oil, T-bone steaks, king salmon, boiled potatoes, salad, apple pie, doughnuts, fried bread, akutuq, and even regular ice cream to the potluck.

We shared stories of the day's events until nightfall, when the reflection of Cape Darby, 150 miles away, floated on the glassy water. The smell of firewood lingered in the air. By 2 A.M., the flames flickered to coals, and fishermen snored in their tents.

In my sleeping bag with my eyes closed, I heard an airplane engine droning in the distance. The passenger must have been a biologist or a fish buyer—definitely not a fisherman. The steady hum of the airplane engine lulled me to sleep where millions of herring were shining like silver dollars in the sunlight.

My Experience on the Blanket Toss

Sandra Russell   Iñupiaq   Kotzebue

•Kotzebue

The message echoed over the intercom. "There will be blanket toss in the gym, coming up shortly." It was Sunday, April 4, 1993. The announcement sounded like any other program offered here at the Anvil Mountain Correctional Center in Nome. I buzzed the tower and said I wanted to participate.

Gregg Nothstein, a young man involved in Native Youth Olympics, had come to demonstrate the blanket toss and to teach others. He is a very handsome Alaska Native, with a muscular body that looks as though he is into body building. His body was very well proportioned. His hair had a spiked look, with razor-short sides. His blue T-shirt had black lettering on it, and he filled it well. Displayed on the back was TUNGWENUK, Gregg's Eskimo name. He wore it proudly. His legs were covered with multicolored and printed pants with elastic around the waist and ankles. This man struck me as an honest person who was walking in two worlds, like a man from the past who is hanging onto his culture while adapting to this modern society.

Tungwenuk spread out his great big blanket made from walrus hides sewn together with black leather. The handles were made of rope that intertwined the holes on the outer edge of the skin.

Although the blanket was made on Little Diomede Island in the Bering Sea, Tungwenuk did most of the repairs and restoration of it himself.

He said when he first got the skin, it was very much like his life. The skin was all folded up tough—hard to manage. The skin was much like his childhood days, Tungwenuk said. He was all bottled up with anger and full of resentment. The blanket was dirty and filthy, he said, just like his life. The stench was so strong, at times he felt like giving up. Tungwenuk compared his blanket's transfor-

Iñupiaq Reggie Joule on the blanket toss. Joule, in 1996 elected a state legislator, is well known throughout Alaska for soaring high on the blanket toss in the World Eskimo Indian Olympics, an annual gathering of indigenous peoples to cooperatively compete in traditional sporting events. Photo by John Creed. 1981.

mation to his personal struggle for sobriety, for alcohol had been destroying his life. His story moved me. Everything Tungwenuk had said about the walrus skin pertained to him in some way.

Naturally, Tungwenuk was the first one we tossed in the air on his blanket. Instead of counting one, two, and three, as we tossed, we all said "Drug free and proud!" We threw Tungwenuk up three times. Each time, we threw him higher. He sailed up and came back down with skill and grace.

I had this gut feeling I was to be next. I thought of Bette Midler when she said, "Alone in the dark with two hundred men. There is a God after all," as she starred in the movie, *Where the Boys Are*. After all, I was the only woman in this institution with approximately two hundred men, but in my case, I felt there was no God. I did not have any faith in myself, much less any trust in these men.

By now, the guys were yelling, "Your turn now, Sandy! Come on, hurry up!" I was faced with a no-win situation, but it's amazing what kind of logic comes to mind under pressure. The logic was, if I don't get on now, I will have to deal with it later. I might as well get it over with, I thought.

As I climbed onto the walrus skin, all of a sudden the blanket did not look as big as I thought it was. We had thrown Tungwenuk way the heck up there, and he outweighed me by a good eighty to ninety pounds. I was overcome with fear. My heart began to beat furiously. I held both my hands over my chest, as if to slow the heartbeats down. My legs were no help at all.

I flashed on the time when I was a child, when I tried to perform an amazing and entertaining act: standing on a rubber ball. I must have looked like an idiot with all my body parts going in every direction, trying to keep my balance. I felt as though I had been coerced into signing my own death warrant. I thought, "Maybe, I'll get lucky and come out of this with only a couple of broken bones." Looking like an idiot didn't seem so bad after all.

It was too late. No way were they going to let me off. All I could do now was close my eyes and pray. I remember hearing the guys say the words, "Drug Free and Proud," as I went screaming into the air. It was a natural-high feeling that I will always remember. Yes, I did manage to land on my feet, but it wasn't over yet. I was afraid of the second toss, because this time I knew they were going to throw me even higher. My pleas to let me off the blanket went unnoticed. Quickly, I sat myself down in the middle of the skin,

Indian style. I was hoping they would get the message that I was dead serious and I wanted off. Instead, they started again, "Drug free and proud." As I went unwillingly into the air, I straightened out my legs and landed on my feet again. After the initial shock was over, I couldn't help smiling proudly. I clenched my fists and said, "Yes!" Nevertheless, there wasn't a guy there who was fast enough to keep me on the blanket for a third try.

It was really neat how we ended the blanket toss. We all grabbed hold of the ropes. We were all working toward sobriety. We all pulled, then gave the skin some slack, then tightened up again quickly. We did this about ten times. Each time it sounded like a heartbeat, a strong and steady heartbeat.

3

Stories of the North

*What I do is just a natural extension of our oral tradition —
storytelling. Really, that's all I do.* — GARY FIFE,
Creek-Cherokee, former host of *National Native News*

Until they began learning the dominant culture's language of English, Native people did not have written languages. Stories, beliefs,
and traditions were passed orally from one generation to the next.
For this reason, storytelling remains to this day a treasured activity
among Native people.

While the Elders' traditional stories and information are being
recorded, translated, and documented on tape and in print, a
younger generation is writing down their own experiences and stories in English. While these cultural changes in language and in
storage of information have taken their toll on the oral tradition,
the value of preserving all of these stories, old and new, cannot be
overemphasized.

Whether relating a humorous story or a tragic one, rural residents
share in life's joys and hardships the same as people everywhere:
We all want to be loved and cherished by the people who are most
important in our lives. Matters of the heart are essentially universal.

For example, losing a loved one changes our lives profoundly, as
Iñupiaq B. J. Criss relates in a story about her brother's valiant
battle with cancer that completely redirected her life. Her brother's
heroism is not unlike the determination to survive displayed in the
story by Berda Willson.

Others write about experiences that hearken back to an earlier
time; they include experiencing spiritual power and yielding it proper respect. Mark Tucker tells of powers that transcend the imagi-
nary ghosts and goblins of Halloween, and in a somewhat similar
vein, Rena Boolowon Booshu tells of feeling the spirit of her late
grandfather. Luci Washington pays homage to her relatives in a potlatch dance.

Geri Reich's story may make us wonder about our fate when we board a small plane, especially in Alaska, where virtually every long-time resident knows someone who has either died in a plane crash or come mighty close to dying. Whether in a plane or on the ground, one cannot afford to take chances in the arctic weather, as we learn alongside writer John Stalker. And, in a comic vein, amid the potential for real danger, one sometimes imagines trouble, as Rachel Sherman relates in "Bear Scare."

In 1990, Alaska made national headlines and was even the subject of ABC's *Nightline* because of—believe it or not—cold weather. This cold weather was unusual enough to freeze solid the water and sewer system in Kotzebue. A writer, Ben Brantley, happened to be one who discovered the problem, so his chapter tells how he helped deal with that particular crisis.

"Stories of the North" are told by "ordinary" rural Alaskans who offer an insight into human experience everywhere.

Brother's Battle with Cancer Sends Sister Home

Blanche Jones "B. J." Criss   *Iñupiaq*   *Kotzebue*

When I used to live along the sandy shores of southern California, it reminded me of home far above the Arctic Circle along Kotzebue Sound in Northwest Alaska. Although I experienced homesickness, I would not express these feelings to anyone.

Sometime during the second week of December in 1984, though, I received a long-distance call that would send me on my journey home.

My brother, Frank Jones, was calling from Ambler on the Kobuk River. His call surprised me, as we rarely communicated, although now and then we would pass on a hello through friends and relatives.

He wasn't feeling well, Frank told me. In fact, he said he had just returned from the local gym where a city league basketball tournament was in full swing, and after only two minutes into the game, he was exhausted. This seemed odd, I thought. My brother always had been considered an all-around athlete.

Frank said he recently had traveled to Kotzebue, our hometown, for a regular check-up at the regional Public Health Service hospital, where doctors had diagnosed him as having ulcers. But even as we talked over the telephone, thousands of miles apart, I sensed that Frank knew something was seriously wrong with him. Having suffered ulcers before and knowing the symptoms, Frank said he realized this was more serious. We hung up.

Frank was in Ambler taking care of his four children, while his wife, Myra, was in Anchorage, about to bear their fifth child. With coaxing from his in-laws at Ambler, and after talking with his wife, Frank flew to Anchorage for a second opinion on his health.

Meanwhile, I returned to my busy life in southern California, getting ready for the Christmas holidays. Frank's call was lost in the holiday rush. In Ventura, two days before Christmas, the poinsettias were in bloom for miles. Christmas cheer filled the air. Being away from family, I always made an extra effort during the holidays for my two boys. The aroma of baked goods filled the house. With flushed cheeks, the boys were wrapping gifts while I tidied up the house.

A few days later, Frank called again. He had just left the doctor's office, where he was told he had cancer. He was scheduled for exploratory surgery on December 26 at the Alaska Native Medical Center in Anchorage. He said he liked the doctor in charge of the surgery because they had both served at the same time in Vietnam.

"How's Myra?" I asked, knowing she was near the phone.

"She should be having the baby any day," Frank replied. As tears welled in my eyes, I asked to speak to Myra.

"Should I fly to Anchorage?" I asked.

"Frank would appreciate it," Myra told me.

Everything suddenly became still and quiet. What I had been doing a few minutes earlier wasn't important anymore. I looked at our Christmas tree. My boys were busy wrapping last-minute presents.

When my husband Criss came home, I told him I should leave immediately for the Los Angeles airport, a two-hour drive. Ultimately, though, we decided it best to leave after the boys opened their presents on Christmas morning.

Reluctantly, I called Frank back and explained my new plans. Frank said he would go to the airport in Anchorage and wait for me. What I'd understood him to say was that when I arrived in Anchorage, he would be waiting for me, which he wasn't. Later, I learned

Iñupiaq Frank Jones,
brother of writer B. J.
Criss, in 1982, when
he served as a member
of the Northwest Arctic
School District Board
of Education. Photo
by John Creed.

that Frank had gone to the airport for a full day right after our phone
call. He probably used this time to think. I'm sure he would have
gone hunting, if he could. That's what most Native Iñupiaq men do
to deal with inner trauma.

As we opened our presents in California on Christmas morning,
Frank called again. He told me God had just sent him a beautiful
Christmas present. They named her Josephine, after a friend who
lived in camp a few miles from their home in Ambler.

On Christmas Day, I headed north to my brother. At Anchorage
International Airport, I called the hospital. I was told that patients
could not receive visitors at that late hour. I could have pressed the
issue, but I think, subconsciously, I wasn't ready to see Frank.

I went to the hospital at eight the following morning. Frank had
been in surgery since 6 A.M. Ironically, when I got there, both Myra
and Frank were in the recovery room for separate surgeries. She
would wake up first, finding herself and Frank together in the recovery room.

As I sat waiting in the visitors' lounge, I made small talk with a
lady who kept herself busy knitting. I talked of my brother in the recovery room. This woman told me that her brother-in-law was also
in the recovery room. Two hours later, we found out we had been
talking about the same person. The woman turned out to be Myra's
oldest sister, Mida. Soon after that, the whole visitors' lounge was
"standing room only." Myra's family had arrived, and so had my parents. It took awhile for my mother to recognize me, as I hadn't seen
her in five years.

After being in the recovery room all day and finally settling into
his private room, Frank had a moment alone with me that evening.
His window overlooked Anchorage. The snowcapped mountains
looked so alive and vibrant, as fresh gigantic snowflakes fell across
the landscape. Brilliant Christmas lights danced on and off
throughout the city. Quietly, Frank said it would be his last Christmas. We said nothing after that. We were both crying. I remember
silently begging God to turn those lights off.

The doctor told Myra that the most Frank had was two months.
The baby, he said, would not know her father. The doctor was
amazed that Frank was still walking.

A few days later, everyone flew to Ambler. I could understand why
Frank loved this small, magnificent village, far above the Arctic
Circle. Outside the house, cords of wood lay neatly stacked, along

with a snowmobile, sled, and dogs. As I entered their home, the smell of firewood filled the living room. Furs from a winter's hunt hung throughout their home.

Each morning, Frank clothed his children, combed their hair, fed them, bundled them for the bitter cold of winter, and walked them to school. Upon his return, he would bring his wife her morning coffee. During the day, his friends would drop in and as the day passed, they'd casually discuss such things as how to brew a good pot of coffee. This was a Frank I'd never experienced before, I thought, as I left the village a few days later.

After my return to California, Myra and Frank decided to fly to the Gersons Institute in Tiajuana, Mexico, for ozone treatments to fight Frank's cancer, which had spread through his lungs, stomach, and liver. They brought along their newborn and Myra's sister, who is a nurse. This method of treatment, which actor Steve McQueen also used, is outlawed in the United States.

I learned a while later that a schoolteacher in Ambler, Barbara McManus, had given Frank ten thousand dollars to do whatever was needed to help fight his deadly disease.

Criss and I drove to Tiajuana from our home in southern California. I wasn't prepared to see Frank, who had lost sixty pounds and now had but a mere ninety pounds clinging to his once athletic frame. Nevertheless, he still spoke and thought clearly. Medically speaking, I think it had to do with his not taking drugs to alleviate his pain. His nurse gave him a coffee enema every few hours to clean out his infected insides, which helped lessen his pain.

Frank knew I could not visit long, so when we found a spare moment, it didn't matter that Criss was beside me.

"Sis, look at you," he said. "You're so healthy but dead. Look at me. I'm sick and I want to live."

I looked at him and inhaled his every word. I noticed his jaw twitching, as it did when he was in deep concentration. Frank had exposed my homesickness.

Criss quietly left the room. Frank and I had a few more quiet minutes together. He said no more.

The following Saturday, Frank's nurse took him outside the clinic for some fresh air. As they sat on a bench outside the clinic, a white dove passed by. Frank's superstitions told him it was a sign to head home.

On the following Sunday morning, I received my last telephone call from Frank.

"Goodbye, sis," he said. "I am going home."

"Good, I'll have your kids meet you in Anchorage," I told him.

"No, I'm going home before I reach Anchorage," he said. "I want to say 'goodbye'." He was tired, he said, and hung up the phone.

Alone with the company of a dial tone, I damned life itself and especially I damned God.

"Why?" I asked. If I could stay angry, I wouldn't lose control. The clock and I visited each other all day.

Late that same afternoon, Frank's nurse called from Anchorage.

During the flight between Seattle and Anchorage, my dear sweet brother had started bleeding through his mouth. He had told his nurse he had to use the restroom.

In the latrine, alone, with a tissue in his hand, Frank died.

Today, each time I walk the beach in my village and smell the ocean, hear its roaring waves, and watch the sea gulls soaring, I think of Frank, and thank him.

I am home now, too, and I want to live.

Halloween Mask

Mark Tucker   Yup'ik   Emmonak

•Emmonak

I first met Alphonsus Pete in the fall of 1970 when my family and I stopped in Sheldon Point, Alaska, on our way home to Emmonak from berry picking. I later got a job in Sheldon Point and got to know Al better when we went hunting and fishing together.

Then, on Halloween 1986, Al came by my house at about 4 P.M. to ask if I wanted to check the hooks that we had set out in the ice to catch fish.

As we left the house, Al suddenly stopped walking.

"Hey, look. What's this?" he asked.

I didn't know what we had found because most of it was hidden underground. We finally got the thing loose with an ax and saw that it was a carved wooden mask. Grass and frozen mud were stuck on it. I brought the mask into my house to thaw it out, and I set it on a shelf above the stove, then went out to check the hooks with Al.

We found no fish on the hooks and went back to my house, where we watched a football game on television. Then trick-or-treaters started coming over. We were having fun until something strange happened to Al. First, blood came flowing out of his nose, then his head started spinning, and his vision doubled. Al went home and I went to bed.

The next evening I got a c.b. call from a city-league basketball team member, asking if I was interested in coming to basketball practice.

I went up to the high school gym, where I went to the men's bathroom to put on my tennis shoes. As I was walking out of the bathroom, blood began to spurt out of my nose. When it stopped bleeding, I was able to play basketball, but about an hour and a half later, while I was still on the court, my head began to reel. Then I started to see double.

I thought of what had happened to Al. It puzzled me that these sudden illnesses had originated the same way.

I went home and slept about two hours. When I woke up, I was looking right at the mask, which was still on the shelf above the stove. I got out of bed, grabbed the mask, and threw it out onto the porch, then tried to go back to sleep, but I didn't sleep the rest of the night.

At 6 a.m., I walked next door where my sister, Amelia, and her husband, Ed, live and told them what happened. "You better call your dad on the phone to ask him what to do with that mask," Ed said.

"I can't use the phone in this condition. Can you make the call for me?" I mumbled.

My dad said Al and I should talk to the oldest man in Sheldon Point about the mask. Later that morning, Al and I arranged to see Andrew Adams, who happened to be Ed's dad.

"The reason you both got sick was that you used an axe to get the mask out of the frozen ground," Andrew explained. "Chopping around the mask with an axe was like hitting the face of the person who once owned that mask.

"That mask was probably worn by a witch doctor or shaman to treat sick people in the early days before there were hospitals nearby. Take that mask away where nobody will find it and tell it you are more than sorry you had ever bothered it," Andrew advised us. "Also, bring a little food and water to put under the ground with the mask."

Later that day, after we'd followed Andrew's instructions, I started to feel much better.

I believe this could have happened to us even if we had found the mask on a day other than Halloween. Somewhere out there on the tundra, there probably are more artifacts that still carry powers of the shaman.

Remembering Grandfather

Rena Boolowon Booshu   *Siberian Yup'ik   Gambell*

During the summer of 1988, I suddenly woke up in the middle of the night to an eerie and unpleasant odor—one that I had never smelled before! Confused whether I had been dreaming or not, I turned over on my side and tried to focus my eyes on the bright red numbers on my digital alarm clock. The numbers read: "4:07 A.M."

The scent that woke me smelled like something left to rot. I slowly sat up and swung my legs over on the sides of the bed. The heavy odor seemed to close in on me. Curiosity took over. My eyes widened. I sniffed around, hoping to find the source of the strange smell. There was nothing.

"Hmm? What could it be?" I wondered. A feeling of sleepiness crept back into my body. Confused, I flopped onto my comfy bed and conked out.

A few weeks passed. Then I had a strange dream: Someone had died, but the funeral was delayed. No one could get any supplies for a coffin. The corpse was starting to smell. Instantly, I woke up to the familiar odor again.

"Why do I keep waking up to an unpleasant odor?" I wondered.

I gave it a lot of thought. This odor matched the one from a few weeks earlier.

"Am I imagining I'm smelling dead people in my dream? No, because the smell was real enough to wake me up. So why do I keep waking up to the smell of decaying bodies? Think! Think!! Waking up to dead bodies in my room? Could it be my grandfather, Samuel?"

After he died in 1985, his body had remained a couple days in this same room. Bad weather had prevented relatives and his coffin from arriving on time for his funeral. His body had started decomposing and had started to smell.

"What's going on? Is he trying to tell me something?" I considered.

I remembered when he passed away: April 25, 1985. It was the last day of Yup'ik Days, a week-long, school-sponsored festival to celebrate our culture in Gambell. The village was recognizing the Elders of the community. I wondered why my grandfather wasn't there. My oldest sister answered that question when she told me Grandpa was leaving for Nome, as he was ill. So when the day was over, I went to see him.

My uncle was taking care of him in a three-bedroom house. His nephews, my parents, and my brothers and sisters were with him. The health aides were also there. I wondered why there were so many people this time.

Usually when he was sick, he'd go to Nome, get treated, and come back in a few days. But this time, he was too weak and had grown doubtful about himself.

Just when the health aides went to report his condition to the doctors in Nome, my grandfather lay down, took two slow and deep breaths, and then stopped breathing. His eyes were still open. When my father closed my grandfather's eyes, he said it was time for grandfather to rest. Grandpa had died of old age without any severe pain. We had known he would leave us sometime and had expected this to happen. We quietly mourned his death.

My grandfather was the oldest person in Gambell at the time of his death — ninety-four years old. When he was a young man, he obeyed his parents, never took any drugs, and had a strong belief in God. He advised us to do as he did, so that we, too, could live a long life.

Being physically fit, he was said to have lifted a heavy rock, which was ten feet wide and ten feet long. He did this by squaring his back with one side of the rock and lifting it upward. Stories also have it that he traveled around all of St. Lawrence Island on foot in only about a week. At first, it spooked me, waking up to the smell of dead people, but not after it dawned on me that I was simply remembering the bittersweet memories of my grandfather's departure. He had loved us all dearly, so I knew he certainly didn't mean to scare me. He was only trying to remind me of his love and of the advice he had given us. After that I never again woke up to the haunting odor. God rest his soul.

Bear Scare

Rachel Sherman   Iñupiaq   Noatak

My sister-in-law and I experienced a "bear scare" one time while we were traveling upriver by boat along with our husbands. We were looking for caribou and for Eskimo potatoes, an edible root that can be found in mouse caches.

The temperature that day rose to only about ten above. We were bundled up in mouton parkas, and we wore our sno-go boots, which were pretty heavy.

We stopped on an island upriver above Noatak. Trees, a shallow creek, and a gravel bar surrounded the island.

My sister-in-law and I got off on the island, and as we started walking, we saw some salmon heads, fish bones, and bear tracks along the trail. This did not stop me from going on, although I noticed my sister-in-law lagged behind, trying to stay close to the shore. I proceeded ahead and stepped on the ground, looking for signs of mouse caches.

I came upon some tall, bushy willows when I heard a noise that sounded like a growl. Without any hesitation, I turned around. My sister-in-law must have read the fear in my eyes, because she turned around, too, and started running. I called out to her, but she never bothered to answer. I bolted.

As chubby as we were, we ran faster than we had ever run before. My sister-in-law had a good head start, but I caught up, then passed her like a speeding bullet. While flying across the tundra, we pictured the poor little mice in their caches beneath us, probably imagining an earthquake was shaking their island.

When we reached the bank of the river, our husbands were fishing from the boat. They heard us run to the shore and looked at us and asked, "What is it?"

Trying to catch my breath, I couldn't utter a word. Sweat was running down my face, yet my throat was dry. My heart was pounding so hard, I had to bend over with my hand on my heart, as if to keep

it from dropping out of place. I kept motioning them to come over with the boat, but they just stared back at us.

When they finally did come across, we got in the boat, rested our poor lungs, and drank water to moisten our throats.

"Maybe what you thought was a bear was just another lady out looking for Eskimo potatoes who coughed to clear her throat," they joked. "Maybe she is running in the opposite direction."

Now every time my husband and I go upriver, I just chuckle to myself when I see the island. By the way, we didn't look for Eskimo potatoes the rest of that day. I told my sister-in-law we could just buy some or not have any at all.

Geese Hunting Provides Valuable Lesson

John Stalker   Iñupiaq   Kotzebue

Last spring when I went out hunting with my Uncle Jeff and his girlfriend, Lena, I learned a valuable lesson about hunting and camping.

We went geese hunting over at the Noatak Flats, the first time I had ever been there. When we got there, my cousins, George and Chip, had been hunting for more than a week. My uncle told me to go to a place and make a blind to hide behind for camouflage. It's difficult for me to make a blind, because I haven't learned all the skills. I tried one with willows.

But making a blind did not work for me, so I decided to move where my uncle Jeff was sitting on a nearby hill. There I saw the two geese he had shot. He told me I could stay with him on the hillside. Within an hour, I got my first goose. As I saw the goose fall, I started running to fetch it. My uncle and his girlfriend just smiled at me when they saw me do that. Later on in the evening, I shot two more geese, and my uncle got a couple more himself.

It was pretty warm during the day, but at dusk, it began to feel a bit cold. Jeff and Lena were ready to head back to town, but I was going to stay at the Noatak Flats overnight. I felt scared, because I had never done that before. George and Chip had already gone

Iñupiaq Rachel Sherman and her husband, Ben, who live in Noatak, Alaska, an Iñupiaq village of 369 residents, fifty-five miles north of Kotzebue on the Noatak River. 1993. Photo by Jim Magdanz.

•Kotzebue

back to town that day, so I would be alone. George had left me his tent to use.

I sat near the tent for awhile and ate some food. I felt uncomfortable outside the tent because it was cold. Also, I had never seen a bear before, and I didn't want to either. Jeff had left me some buckshot shells in case a bear came along, but I didn't feel especially safe. Also, there was a fox running around.

I felt uncomfortable inside the tent because it, too, was cold. I finally fell asleep late that night, and I have never been so cold in my life. I never got much sleep because I kept thinking of bears, and I didn't know if the fox would come around. If someone had seen me, they would have known I was scared because I had my gun right next to me the whole night with the buckshot shells loaded.

I woke up early in the morning, ready to go home to Kotzebue. Jeff had told me that he would be back, that I was supposed to stay and wait for him. But I couldn't stay out on the flats any longer.

When I got back to Kotzebue, it was about 11:00 A.M., and my uncle was still sleeping. I woke him up. He was surprised to see me so soon. From this experience, I learned more about camping out and knowing what to do next time, such as taking all the warm clothing I can.

Dancing at a Traditional Potlatch

St. Michael

Luci Washington   *Yup'ik   St. Michael*

About three hundred and fifty adults and children packed the community hall in the neighboring community of Stebbins, Alaska, for our Traditional Annual Potlatch. As I entered the building, I stopped for a moment to gaze at what was before me.

"Wow, am I really going to perform before all these people?" I thought.

I scanned the room, looking for people I recognized: Elders, adults, children, and infants. Most of the people at the hall were Natives, but a couple of blacks and a few white people mingled among the crowd, too. The Elders were talking in their Native tongue. The sounds of laughter and babies crying filled the hall, and I heard someone calling out a name.

All the Native drummers wore T-shirts and faced the crowd. Three pitchers of water were perched in front of them to quench their thirst. The leader gave the signal, and the singers began chanting a Yup'ik song in a soft tone, blending in with the stroke of the drums. A drummer pulled a handkerchief out of his pocket to wipe away his oozing sweat.

A six-year-old, with both her great-grandparents at her side, stood on a beaver skin in front of the crowd, bending her knees to the beat of the drum. She smiled at the crowd in a bashful way. Their kuspuks matched identically, each made with pink material, with red hearts sewn on the flounce and on the front pockets. Their headdresses were made of wolverine skin and reindeer whiskers and were trimmed with Eskimo beads. Their fans were identical, too, made from reindeer whiskers and woven grass. The girl danced to the song her great-grandmother made up for her. The song translated into English was, "As I'm growing up."

The smell of cigarettes floated into the hall as the doors were opened to circulate the heated air. The various smells of perfume, shaving lotion, body odor, and the smell of new soles on mukluks certainly didn't mix, but the cool air was a pleasure as it went by.

There were twenty dances scheduled for the night. As gifts were passed out between the dances, young children ran around among the crowd to get attention.

Once the dancing began, the Elders who had come into the hall with the aid of a cane or crutches were no longer helpless. The arthritic joint was forgotten. Instead, their minds were drifting to the past, lost in the chanting and beating of the drum. Their arms were swaying as fast as the drums were beating.

Someone sang a happy tune, bringing the dancers to life. Tiny beads of sweat formed on their foreheads. They wore mukluks made of sealskin, with bleached shoe laces and beaver tops.

One group, the Comedian Dancers, were all dolled up with bright red lipstick, rosy cheeks, and blue eye shadow. This dance was dedicated to a distant relative, a man whom the dancers teased to come down and dance with them. As the dancers continued to tease him, he only hollered, "Bumyuq!" That meant they had to do the dance all over again. This continued until the dancers were exhausted.

My dance was the last one for the night. I stood before the crowd, a little nervous, sweat seeping out from the palms of my hands. The chanting started out low and slow, my knees bending to the beat of the drum.

My headdress was unique, with old beads sewn to the wolverine skin, and my kuspuk was made from a light blue material, with red and blue rickrack trim. My Yup'ik name, Nacuguniaq, was sewn across the pocket with blue rickrack. My dance fans were made from caribou whiskers and woven grass, also with my name written on them. Three yards of material rested on my right arm, which I would use to dance on since I didn't have a skin to stand on.

When the signal to dance was given, I dropped the material to the floor and began dancing, slowly at first. Gradually, the beat got faster. As I danced harder and faster, the fear and nervousness disappeared; instead, happiness and excitement flowed within me. Happy tears formed in my eyes. A tear dropped for my late grandmother, who wasn't there to watch me dance. The dance got livelier and faster. Then, the singers and drummers stopped for a while, and my friends and relatives joined in the dance.

Before I knew it, the dance was over. A part of me was everywhere, sharing happy moments with old friends. I walked up to one of the Elders I liked and gave the material to her. Then, my family helped me pass out gifts to the public. I glanced at the audience one last time. I knew they were happy.

So was I.

Small Aircraft Flight Turns Silent after Frightening Experience

Geri Reich   Iñupiaq   Kotzebue

Al's Gals, our local softball team, was waiting impatiently at the Kotzebue airport for the pilot who was to fly us from Kotzebue in Northwest Alaska to Valdez in south-central Alaska for the annual state softball tournament.

Our sponsor, state senator Al Adams, had arranged for part of the team to fly down in a small, six-seater Bush plane. The other players had already gone down on an Alaska airlines jet that morning. We planned to meet later in Valdez.

We had worked hard all summer long to make money for the trip. Bake sales, car washes, and raffles took most of our time as we tried to make enough for all fourteen of us to attend the tournament.

The pilot finally came and introduced himself. He looked a little tired, as if he had stayed up late the previous night. Nevertheless, everyone quickly threw their bags into the plane, climbed aboard, and fastened their seat belts. As we took off from Kotzebue, little did we realize that this flight would remain more prominent in our minds in the coming years than the tournament itself.

On the airplane, Tubby, our assistant coach, eagerly suggested we all play a game of cribbage.

"We've all got to draw on the jacks to see who gets to play the first game," said Annie, our team shortstop.

A look of triumph spread across Tubby's face as he drew a jack of clubs. I then drew a jack of hearts and settled back into my seat as the other four huddled around the deck of cards, fervently wishing they too would draw a lucky card.

"I've got one," cried Tina, Annie's sister and our third baseman.

"I'm in, too," said Annie. "Let's see who deals."

The two who got left out, Tooten and Joyce, looked on with interest as the game got under way. The lowest card drawn decides the dealer. Annie drew the six of diamonds, with Tubby drawing a six of clubs. It was my turn to draw from the deck.

"Cherry, don't get another six," Tubby whispered to me.

"I won't," I said with apprehension growing inside me.

I slowly picked a card and held it face down in front of me. With trepidation, I turned it over. There it was, a six of spades!

Everyone's eyes got wide with disbelief and fear, as three sixes in a row means bad luck. The four of us simultaneously shoved the cards back into their case.

Silence filled the cabin. No longer were we enthusiastic about the trip. The hours passed. Most everyone fell asleep to the drone of the plane's engine.

I awoke with Tubby shaking me, pointing out at the dense fog surrounding the plane. I glanced around the cabin and made sure everyone else was awake. Whispering to one another, we looked to the pilot for some kind of assurance. He gave no indication of any dilemma.

High mountains passed by as we flew in and around them. A dark shape appeared to our left. It instantly disappeared. It was another plane!

All of a sudden, we dropped vertically. A mountain loomed directly in front of us! We quickly accelerated, scaling the mountain's slope, looking for any small opening.

The pilot made a sharp turn to the right and finally, familiar-looking houses, trees, and cars came into sight far below.

As we landed on the runway, the FAA flight controller yelled through the radio, "They just landed."

The plane taxied to a stop in front of a huge building. The pilot, never saying a word to us during the whole flight, unbuckled his belt, jumped out of the plane, and ran.

We all sat there for a while in the plane's cabin, slowly absorbing what had just happened.

A First-Hand Account of the Kotzebue's Water System Freeze-Up

Benjamin Uvigaq Brantley   Iñupiaq   Kotzebue

On February 10, 1990, the temperature in Kotzebue dipped to minus forty degrees.

I was on call that evening for the Kotzebue water and sewer department. The local police called me to tell me about a frozen waterline at House Number 626. I responded and installed a thaw box. As I hopped back into the public works van, a man ran up to me.

"My water is starting to freeze," he said. "I never had this problem before."

"I'll bring a thaw box over to your trailer," I told him.

With a spade shovel, I chipped away the foam around the water loop underneath his home to get to the dielectrics (which stops the flow of electricity to the plumbing inside the house). But I could not thaw out his water line because, apparently, he was missing a ground strap at the water main that lets the electricity circulate through the ingoing and outgoing copper lines.

Meanwhile, I kept getting calls from people telling me, "My next door neighbor's water is frozen, too." I started to suspect the prob-

lem lay at Sixth Street and Wolverine Drive, uptown, where we had gotten our first reports of frozen water lines.

I drove back to public works and got a hold of the water plant operator to see if there was flow from the uptown water loop. When we went inside the plant, we looked at the water meter, and the needle was at a standstill. It didn't even budge. That meant water wasn't returning back to the plant.

Around 11:00 P.M., top officials from the city arrived at the water plant, wondering what they could do to solve what had become an increasingly serious problem. While they were talking over what could be done about the situation, the number of frozen waterlines increased throughout the night. The police station and water plant kept receiving calls from the uptown residents during the early morning hours.

At 8:00 A.M. sharp, the phones began to ring nonstop and continued throughout the day. By the end of the workday, some ninety frozen waterlines in Kotzebue had been reported.

The city declared an emergency. People were hired from out of town to get things organized during the disaster. Also, many men were hired locally to try to save the water main. Two crews of about twenty-five men split the job into twelve-hour shifts.

Iñupiaq Ben Brantley
and his wife, Laura.
Kotzebue, Alaska,
1992. Photo by Jim
Magdanz.

The work started to pile up. All day long, you could hear the noise of jackhammers that sounded like machine guns in the distance. Contractors' backhoes were also scratching at Kotzebue's frozen, rocky streets. As the operators dug holes all around the frozen loop uptown, it looked as if World War III had begun. Hydroflush trucks flushed out frozen sewer lines, a steam truck from North Pole, Alaska, thawed out the frozen loop, and a specially designed truck began delivering water around the clock.

The biting cold pushed steady plumes of steam out of local residents' stove stacks, making the houses look like awkward locomotives barreling down the tracks. As the freezing weather persisted, we wondered if the cold spell would ever lift. At the work sites, icicles clung to the workers' mustaches, and some of us were getting the shivers from the sub-zero temperatures.

A few days later, water finally began circulating again through the uptown loop except for Greyling to Sixth Streets, between Turf Street and Ptarmigan Way, the area where the frozen water main had shattered.

Next, some new, six-inch, insulated arctic pipe arrived and was fused together and installed above the ground as a temporary water main. The following summer, we disconnected the temporary arrangement and buried the new pipe permanently.

We worked long hard hours to restore running water so that local residents once again could wash their dirty clothes and dishes, as well as take showers at home and flush their toilets. However, residents in at least fifty homes in Kotzebue had to wait patiently before water flowed again out of their faucets.

We all have to live with experiences like this in the Arctic. We must expect the unexpected.

Rescue on the Trail of Ice

Berda Willson   Iñupiaq   Nome

*Berda Willson did not want to give her son's name in this story because it might be "a bad omen."

As my eldest son mushed his dog team along the trail on the Bering Sea ice, he felt strong and alive as the warm lifeblood pulsed through his young veins.* Feeling invincible, he harbored no thought of the impending danger that lay just ahead on the trail. Although just twenty-four years old at the time, this experienced young dog musher had run his own team since he was fifteen. The weather was cold on this day, thirty below zero, but there was no wind. For mushers raised on the typically windswept coast of Northwest Alaska, it was a fair day for running dogs. Despite years of wilderness travel by dog team, my son did not anticipate the ordeal he was about to encounter.

He had run his dogs over this ice trail many times. The ice, favored by both dog mushers and snowmachiners, always made a nice smooth trail. Cape Nome jutted directly out into the Bering Sea's Norton Sound in deep water, making it hard to get around the cape without going out onto the ice to avoid the nearly impassable huge granite boulders along the shore. Just the night before, my son had used this same trail to transport his younger brother to their camp at Nuuk some twenty miles east of Nome. He was returning alone the following day for more supplies. On this early February day, the sun would not be rising until almost 11 o'clock in the morning. My son peered through the inky blackness, barely able to distinguish the ghostly shapes of the snow-covered ice hummocks in the distance. The dogs knew the trail well, though, and their driver was confident in their ability. No sign of danger offered any reason to fear for their safety this day.

As my son rounded Cape Nome, the horizon expanded, diffused in a reddish, orange-pink glow. The cold winter sun would soon be rising for a brief few hours. The wind freshened. He felt the chill on his exposed face, so he quickly adjusted the wolverine ruff on his parka to curl closer around his face. He called the dogs up to hurry them along. Sounds of the comforting hiss of sled runners on ice and the rhythm of the panting dogs lulled him as they moved toward Nome, still some twelve miles in the distance. His sled was a handsome twelve-foot freighter he had made himself, a skill taught in the traditional way by Iñupiaq Elder Fred Armstrong. My son had chosen a good heavy hardwood to withstand the rough terrain of the ice and hard-packed snow of Northwest Alaska. Today he was running just ten dogs, including three-year-old pups. The team was still moving along at a steady pace.

Every so often my son pushed with his foot to give the dogs a little help. Something didn't feel quite right, though. His foot felt like it was sinking slightly with each pump. Casually, he glanced back at his trail. With alarm mounting, he could see water welling up from his footprints. He was on thin ice!

"Gee! Gee!" my son yelled at his leaders, commanding a turn to the right toward the solid shore. The dogs did turn sharply, but the runners dug in, and the sled carrying the musher plunged into the icy waters, dragging the back four dogs with it.

Instantly, my son thought of cutting the dogs loose as the numbing water closed around him. "Where is my knife? Where is my knife?" he asked himself frantically.

He couldn't lift his heavy parka high enough in the freezing water to reach his knife, and he knew he needed it to get to the shore ice before he could ever pull the dogs to safety.

My son tried desperately to crawl up onto the thin ice, but it kept breaking under him. Panic hit. He lunged and thrashed with his young dogs in the freezing water, as the other dogs looked on helplessly. Cold and shock numbed his body and slowed his movements. He was becoming increasingly weaker. Despite all his frantic effort, my son managed to calm himself. He tried to think rationally.

"If I can throw myself up on the ice, maybe it won't break," he thought.

His strength almost gone, my son heaved himself up on the thin ice and began rolling toward shore. When he thought it was safe, he stood up, only to break through again!

"Please, please, let someone help me," he pleaded silently. "I don't want to die." Somehow my son managed to get back up onto the treacherous ice again, and he continued rolling toward the shore ice once again.

As he rolled, he spotted a lone snowmachine bobbing toward him on the shore ice, pulling a canoe behind it.

"Am I dreaming this?" my son thought to himself.

Stinging tears of joy and hope froze on the young musher's face. He recognized his rescuer, the kind, gentle Herbie Wilkalkia, a fellow Iñupiaq he had known all his young life. Herbie and his wife Bertha were the only human inhabitants for miles. The elderly man had been keeping watch and listening for the sound of snowmachines from his home up on the hill about a quarter-mile away. Herbie knew the ice had moved out late the night before, leaving only a thin, unsafe layer, despite the frigid temperatures. Herbie had readied his canoe and snowmachine in case misfortune should strike some unfortunate traveler. Incredibly though, Herbie had been listening for the roar of a snowmachine. He almost missed seeing the young musher and his silently moving dog team.

By this time, the musher's clothes had frozen stiff. He could barely move. Herbie, a fairly small man, also was plagued with a weak heart. My son stands six-foot-four and weighs 190 pounds.

"I cannot save the dogs without your help," Herbie told the musher. "You must leave the dogs and come with me to change your clothes."

The six dogs from the front of the team stood on the dangerous thin ice as motionless as statues, as if they knew they dared not move. The four dogs still in the icy water cried out and thrashed wildly.

The musher had no choice but to go with Herbie back to his house to get out of the clothes that were imprisoning him in a cocoon of ice. They removed the young musher's frozen parka, leaving it on the shore. Shivering violently, although now moving more freely, the young musher climbed into the sled that had carried the canoe. Herbie quickly started his machine, and they headed for his warm cabin. The sound of the snowmachine drowned out the wails of the four dogs that had to be left behind to the mercy of the freezing water.

Herbie's wife, Bertha, had prepared hot cocoa, tea, and coffee as she waited anxiously for the safe return of her husband and the still unknown traveler. With alarm, she recognized my son and quickly went about helping him out of his frozen clothes and into some of Herbie's. Still shivering violently, my son quickly took massive gulps of hot cocoa. The couple rapidly rummaged through their belongings and found a snowsuit almost large enough to fit, although the too-small clothes gave my son an almost comical appearance. A pair of Herbie's largest mukluks with heavy wool socks, hand-knit by Bertha, had to suffice for footwear instead of the normal size thirteen my son wears.

When Herbie and my son returned to the team, the front six dogs were still waiting calmly, but only one of the dogs in the water was still moving. She was the oldest; the three pups had died from the cold and shock.

Herbie and my son used the canoe in the rescue like an iceboat to reach the dogs and sled. They had returned with a rope that was long enough to attach to the sled and pull it to safety with the use of the snowmachine. Incredibly, after retrieving his sled and the remaining seven dogs, the musher then continued on to Nome.

Herbie wished the young musher a safe passage to Nome, politely accepting my son's heartfelt thanks. He then calmly went back to his home and his waiting wife. Each man silently and sadly acknowledged the loss of the dogs, and each accepted without comment the danger they had both survived. Although Herbie was a true hero, typical of Iñupiaq Eskimos, he viewed such heroic deeds as just another day in his life. Herbie was not looking for notoriety when he saved my son's life, and the lives of most of his dogs. He only sought the satisfaction of helping others who needed his help.

Herbie died quietly in his sleep a year or so after this heroic deed, and his loving wife Bertha followed a few years later, but they will live on forever in the hearts and minds of the young musher and his grateful family.

My son never used that ice trail again.

4

Formal Schooling

*The books told how bad the Indians had been to the white
men—burning their towns and killing their women and children. But I had seen white men do that to Indians. We all
wore white man's clothes and ate white man's food and went
to white man's churches and spoke white man's talk. And
so after a while we also began to say Indians were bad.*
—SUN ELK, Taos Pueblo, writing in the late 1800s

In the words of Lakota writer Vine Deloria Jr., education for Native
Americans has been a "major area of conflict and concern" since
the first contact with Europeans. For Alaska's indigenous peoples,
conflict first arose over the near extinction of Native languages at
the hands of early educators. Conflict continues over textbooks and
curricula that gloss over, ignore, or misrepresent Native people.
Despite the many failures of Western-style schooling, the dominant culture's education has in recent decades proved a valuable
tool in achieving more self-determination for Native people.

Alaska's checkered history of Western education begins with
missionaries. Some successes, at least conditional ones, can be
counted among these early experiences. For instance, as far back as
Russia's ownership of Alaska, amid the subjugation of the Aleuts
and exploitation of their resources by Russian invaders, some mea-
sure of reprieve arrived with missionary Ivan Veniaminov in 1824.
While converting the Aleut people to the Russian Orthodox religion, Veniaminov also learned their language, developed an Aleut
alphabet and grammar for the language, created vocational schooling, sought better treatment for the people, and recorded valuable
information. Later, Alaska's best-known missionary, Presbyterian
Sheldon Jackson, in the late 1800s sought federal support for
Native education, but in opening the territory to various churches
(for instance, the Friends Church settled Northwest Alaska, the
Moravians the Kuskokwim region), he gave missionaries license to
dismantle not only ten thousand years of spirituality but traditional

songs and dances associated with them. Some of the various organized religions that carved up Alaska in the late 1800s under Sheldon Jackson's direction have in recent years publicly apologized for the resultant loss of cultural practices such as Eskimo singing and dancing.

Eventually, both federal and territorial governments took over responsibility for schooling Alaska's Native peoples. Under government auspices, educational settings included everything from elementary schools that went up to fourth grade, to those that went through eighth grade, to boarding schools operated by the Bureau of Indian Affairs, to "separate but equal" segregated schools operated by the territory. After a landmark 1975 case that said students had a constitutional right to a K–12 education in their home community, small rural high schools were built across the state. While in the past the aim had often been assimilation, more recently the aim has been to keep the children close to their cultural heritage in their home communities. Contributors to this volume, who were born during the "baby boom," typically completed their education at home until high school, when they would leave for a distant boarding school.

While some regard the experience of leaving for boarding school disruptive of family life, especially of their cultural roots, their language, and their subsistence activities, even today others feel such an arrangement was preferable to small rural schools where access to a broad curriculum and a variety of teachers were lacking. Today some young people continue to choose to go away to boarding school, for instance, to Mt. Edgecumbe High School in Sitka, Alaska, or Chemawa Indian School in Oregon. (An interesting footnote to Alaska history is that Native political leaders attribute much of their ability to unify the various Native groups around the state—particularly in seeking passage of the 1971 Alaska Native Claims Settlement Act—to the fact that many got to know each other while together at boarding school.)

Perhaps the most succinct expression of the confusion wrought by the various educational systems and policies over the years can be found in the oft-cited observation that "today the government wants us to learn our language (through bilingual programs), which the teachers used to beat out of us."

Perhaps the most deplorable legacy of Western education is the loss of Native languages. Today, out of a population of twelve thousand Iñupiaq in the Northwest and North Slope regions of Alaska, roughly four thousand speak the language; few of those are children. The language of southwestern Eskimos, Central Yup'ik, has a firmer hold. A 1980 estimate put the proportion of speakers at fourteen thousand out of seventeen thousand, including many children. However, a current estimate shows the number of Central Yup'ik speakers dropping to closer to twelve thousand.

While writer James Gooden was not physically beaten as a boy in an urban Alaska school, he was verbally and emotionally mistreated. His tale of blatant discrimination seems outlandish today, for who could believe that a Fairbanks schoolteacher would have asked a timid young Eskimo student if "his kind" still rubbed noses when they made love? "I could never forget something like that," says James. "I remember it like it happened yesterday."

Despite the tragic loss of language for so many, others fortunately fared better. In her job in Kotzebue for NANA Regional Corporation, Hannah Paniyavluk Loon often translates and interprets Iñupiaq and English for people. Her first language is Iñupiaq, but she writes in this chapter about her great affection also for village English, an efficient oral language, in which "I structure my sentences any way I desire."

In contemporary Alaska, language knowledge now extends to computers. Native people find themselves needing to be on the cutting edge of technology just like people everywhere, as Sonny Harris explains in his piece defining a computer nerd.

Lucy Daniels's selection describes the sensation of starting school "ice cold," as if without a compass, that left her not only having difficulty identifying north from south and east from west but also in comprehending the myriad of cultural differences between her upbringing and Western schooling. Also, read in Georgianna Lincoln's "Lack of True American Indian History in Textbooks" all about why some Native Americans don't appreciate the short shrift they've received in America's school textbooks. She also touches on how educational institutions' research arm sometimes reaches beyond the bounds of scholarship into desecration of Native history. Indeed, educational, research, and scientific institutions themselves have not always acted in the best interests of Native people, as we learn in Sheila Gregg's contribution about Project Chariot, an example of deception by the scientific and academic communities in the Atomic Age.

Writer Ruthie Sampson describes a feeling akin to Georgianna's and Lucy's when she became aware of the lack of learning about "the Eskimos" in school. She goes on to offer us an insight into why a Native woman would dedicate her professional career to incorporating traditional Iñupiat language and skills into local schools. People on the forefront of this critical battle to save the language and cultural traditions, such as Sampson, are also recording cultural traditions. Sampson has published several books on the local culture while living in Kotzebue with her husband, a competitive dog musher, and their four children.

Finally, in this collection of opinions about formal schooling, writer Berda Willson relates the story of her long-determined road to completing a college degree, an example of the traditional Native value of hard work, as well as a testament to the value of education, despite more than a century of at-best erratic educational policy.

•Kiana

Iñupiaq Relates Hard Times in Elementary School in the 1950s

James Gooden   Iñupiaq   Kiana

I felt strange, lost in this new setting: sixth grade in Fairbanks, 1959.

I was instructed by the new teacher to occupy the last desk at the back of the room. Students filled about nine other desks in front of me.

All the students had to stand and introduce themselves. When my turn came, I felt a silence creep into the air as the teacher strolled over to the large classroom windows.

"My name is Ronald Gooden," I began.

"What kind of name is Ronnie Gooden?" the teacher asked.

I didn't respond. I didn't know how. I just stood there.

"Okay," she continued. "Can you speak English?"

"Yes," I replied, puzzled by the slight grin on her face.

"What race do you belong to, Ronnie?" she asked, facing the other students. I looked into the faces of some of the students and cleared my throat.

"I'm an Eskimo," I said.

"Do you live in an igloo?" the teacher asked.

"No," I replied.

I was beginning to choke up, afraid she would ask yet another question.

"Do your kind still eat raw meat?" she asked.

The teacher walked toward me. I began to stiffen, pinching the seams along the sides of my pant legs.

"Yes, sometimes," I replied, as some of the students began to giggle.

"Well, Ronnie, tell me this. Do you still rub noses when you make love?" the teacher asked.

I began to shake a little, almost to the point of wanting to cry. Fortunately, I remained in control.

"No, not that I know of," I replied.

The teacher went on with her student orientation about school operations. She explained the rules—for the class, in the school, on the playground, and on the use of the rest room. She thumbtacked the gym schedule to the bulletin board, indicating the days and times the gym was to be used. She explained the school lunch program, the cost for the lunch, and the weekly menu. School books were handed out; their arrangement in our desks, she commanded, was not to be changed.

Despite my embarrassment that first day, I was determined to do well. At first, I earned fairly good grades, which surprised our teacher. I had always tried to do my best, as my mother and father had told me. I became the class artist, drawing head figures of presidents. Lincoln, Adams, and Jefferson were my favorites. I played basketball, becoming center for the school team, the Hunter Hornets.

As the school year wore on, our teacher began to carry a ruler or yardstick around the classroom while we worked. She clenched the ruler in one hand, rapping it against the palm of the other. If she was displeased about anything, she would let us know by hitting the top of our desks without warning.

As we worked, she would pick up worksheets from our desks. She seemed to pick mine more often than others. Mine always seemed to have the most mistakes, which she always made sure the rest of the class knew. When she spoke to me, her voice always seemed to get a little higher than usual, as one foot tapped the floor.

My friend, Ronald Sheppard, and I, sensing unfairness toward me, devised a plan to find out if our teacher was grading my papers properly. Doing identical work, we simply would change the wording around a little.

On average, Ronald was a B+ student. We tested our plan in American history, in which I had always received lower grades than Ronald, even though I didn't feel I deserved lower grades. We switched papers. I had Ronald's and he took mine. We passed the switched papers in.

Surprise! I received a low grade, only it was really his paper. Was he shocked! I got my paper from Ronald. I had received a B. I was not shocked.

Ronald and I took our papers to our basketball coach, Mr. Bill Donowick, who brought it to the principal's attention. Our teacher was notified. We both got in trouble for playing a trick on the teacher and received zeros for that paper. Ronald was then moved to the front of the class. I was to remain in the same spot. My grades improved, but essentially remained at the B-minus to D range.

Despite the odds, I tried extra hard to improve or correct my work, even though I knew that when the teacher approached my desk, her fists resting on her hips, I would lose. Her piercing eyes would glare at me through those wire-rimmed glasses as she stood slightly bent over my desk.

"What are you doing?" she would ask.

"I'm doing my work over again," I would reply.

"No, you've already gotten a zero on the one I threw away in the trash can, and there is no make-up for sloppy work," she would say.

Time passed. I bore through the ordeal as best I could. In fact, the teacher's throwing of my papers into the trash eventually tapered off to only twice a week.

During reading, though, others could either sit or stand when they read to the class. I was required to stand, and to remain standing after reading.

I hated Fridays, for these were the days that test papers were graded and placed on top of the teacher's desk. My paper always seemed to be on the top. Red slashes always marked my whole sheet.

Some students began to dislike this teacher. We gave her a nickname because she reminded us of the nice little old lady cartoon character in "Sylvester and Tweetie," only the opposite. Our teacher always wore the same black dress, or at least it appeared so. She also wore a black hat, never taking it off. She wore those high, thick-heeled, below-the-ankle shoes of the mid-1940s.

I started to play hooky. Some days I played sick so as not to go to school. My absences just kept increasing.

Finally, report-card day at the end of the school year arrived. I read mine: "TO BE RETAINED IN THE SIXTH GRADE NEXT YEAR." I sat in silence, not looking at anyone. The bell rang; then came the dash for the door. I headed for the first trash can on the playground, where I watched the torn pieces of green paper hit the bottom of the barrel.

Summer passed. The following September, I returned to the same school, but I was assigned to the classroom across the hall from the one the previous year—a different classroom, a different teacher.

I wasn't assigned to the back row anymore, and I began earning good grades. When I was called upon to do something in class, the teacher encouraged me with a smile. I grew a lot that year.

Mrs. Danforth, in her mid-forties, of average height, was very pretty with a pleasant personality. Her shoulder-length light brown hair, mixed with some gray, complemented her light complexion. She always wore pretty dresses or skirts with colorful blouses. A scent of flowers filled the air whenever she entered the classroom or whenever she passed by our desks.

Thanks to Mrs. Danforth, I walked a little taller. I can still say a few of the French words she taught me.

I will never forget her.

Lack of True American Indian History in Textbooks

Rampart •

Georgianna Lincoln   *Athabascan*   *Rampart*

When I was a little girl, my mother taught me that our Athabascan tribe contains many subtribes, dialects, and customs, each having its own chief and set of Elders.

Imagine my surprise to read the following words in a history textbook called *America, America* and written for tenth graders in Ameri-

can schools: "A tribe is a group that is united by a common history, follows the same customs, and is ruled by the same chief or group of Elders. The people of each tribe speak the same language, and have the same religion."

Unfortunately, this inaccuracy is mild compared to some of the other things I discovered while reviewing how Native Americans are portrayed in the history textbooks used in our schools, and how they have been regarded by society. It's no wonder that some of the general public, and to some extent, even a former president of the United States, continue to think of Native Americans as "savages."

One textbook, for example, a lower elementary social studies text called Family and Friends, depicts a Native family of four dressed in Western clothing and lighting their daughter's birthday cake amid modern napkins, china dishes, silverware, and ornate furniture.

This is not to say some Indians are not Westernized, but I don't believe this would be the image that most Native Americans would want to give American children who are just learning about American Indians. Instead of middle America, why not show an Indian family in a natural setting, surrounded by extended family members in a village or on a reservation?

When American children reach the seventh grade, they may read the history text, People, Places and Change, which devotes but one page to American Indians, of which an illustration of a Pueblo takes up half the page.

Considering that Native Americans were the first people on this continent, it should stand to reason that American Indian history, art, folk tales, literature, religion, and language would be accorded the proper coverage, respect, and accuracy in textbooks. No such luck.

On the college level, a freshman history class uses a textbook called The American Nation. Just four of 972 pages are dedicated to the history of Indians during the late 1800s. Students learn only that Indians went to war over losing their land. I do not believe this goes far enough. For example, this history text does not tell who American Indians are. How did they live? What was an Indian community like? What was it like to be born into an Indian family? What was their relationship to other tribes? How did they determine boundaries? What was their means of transportation before the influx of white settlers? How was the chief selected? What were the various roles of family members?

Interestingly, a timeline in *The American Nation* depicts historical events for this period, but not one single Indian name or event is recognized.

Unfortunately, few history texts being published even today reflect any meaningful change. For example, the text *From Columbus to Aquarius* was termed "controversial" by an instructor because it revealed "too much" of the Indians' history, dilemma, and treatment. The first chapter of this text, for example, gives the history of Indian culture, not wars. Also, a listing of chronological dates and events of Indian cultural cycles is, indeed, refreshing, if "controversial."

Next, the author of this text writes a mock story headed, "The Only Good Indian Is a Dead Indian!" The story depicts a cowboy-and-Indian covered wagon scene, with Indians scalping the white man and the white man shooting the Indians, and with the cavalry (of course) driving the Indians back to their little piece of the earth. This satire, I believe, points out the unfair treatment of Native Americans in American history textbooks.

Moreover, the author states: "Unknown or forgotten are the many accomplishments and contributions of the Indian before, during and after the arrival of the white man. . . . The American Indian was really the first explorer, colonist, and conqueror of the North American continent—the first American." I believe that this is really the crux of the matter. If all history books were to give credit to American Indians for all their accomplishments, American society would not be so ignorant on the subject. But we are. Consequently, the negative stereotyping of Indians, which we are taught and which we teach our children, perpetuates itself from one generation to the next.

Indeed, many people continue to think of Indians as "savages" with no feelings. *National Geographic* highlighted the problem in its March 1989 issue. The magazine reported on a historical Indian burial ground desecrated by grave robbers searching for Indian artifacts that had been buried with the dead. In fact, *National Geographic* reported that even whole skulls still are sold at non-Indian swap meets. Incredibly, some sources quoted in this article see grave diggers as collectors of history, not destroyers of it. Where might this mentality come from? I suggest, to a large extent, from school textbooks.

National Geographic did not let archaeologists off the hook, either. With bones scattered over a wide burial area that had been disturbed, archaeologists collected them for study, the magazine re-ported, then returned them to the Indians for reburial.

"What if this were a white cemetery that had been desecrated? Would the archaeologists be bagging the disturbed bones and grave goods to take them for study at museums and universities?" asked an American Indian interviewed for the *National Geographic* story.

Is this a result of an ignorance of or insensitivity to Indian history by those who may have read the school history texts previously mentioned?

Ronald Reagan, in response to a question from Moscow State University students late in his presidency, said that it might have been better to have forced Native Americans to enter Western cul-ture instead of living in a "primitive life-style" on reservations.

Again, Mr. Reagan was perpetuating the cowboy and Indian im-age: the cowboy to the rescue and the Indian doing the scalping. If America's former highest government official does not know the difference, what more can we expect from the students in class-rooms? What textbooks did Ronald Reagan read in school?

American history textbooks must give a fair, historical perspective of American Indians, not a vision of half-naked savages scalping people and burning wagons. They must portray the Indian as the first explorer, the first colonist, the first conqueror of the North American continent—THE FIRST AMERICAN!

Henry S. Commager, the famous historian, once wrote: "A people without a history is like a man without memory; each generation would have to learn everything anew—make the same discoveries, invent the same tools and techniques, wrestle with the same prob-lems, commit the same errors."

American Indians ask for no less. American Indians do not want their children growing up with an image of the first Americans as brutal savages.

Teller Misled Alaskans on Project Chariot

Sheila Gregg   Iñupiaq   Deering

Project Chariot was a scheme by the federal government's Atomic Energy Commission to create a deep-water port between Kivalina and Point Hope in Northwest Alaska in the late 1950s and early 1960s by detonating up to six thermo-nuclear bombs.

The atomic scientist Edward Teller misled the people of Alaska about the dangers of Project Chariot. He was not intellectually honest with Alaskans about many aspects of the project, including the amount of money that would be spent in the state, about his claim of having an open mind about where to locate the project, and about the size and shape of the harbor that was to be made at Ogotoruk Creek, the proposed site.

According to Dan O'Neill's book, *The Firecracker Boys*, Teller told the public that Project Chariot would help the Alaska economy because the federal government would be spending two-thirds of the Project's $5 million budget in Alaska on making the harbor. Nevertheless, Teller still had trouble justifying the project itself. He said he welcomed suggestions, giving Alaskans the impression that if they wanted a harbor in another place besides Cape Thompson near Point Hope, he would try making one elsewhere in Alaska. In internal AEC memos, however, Teller wrote at the time that the AEC indeed wanted the harbor made at Cape Thompson, according to *The Firecracker Boys*, and Teller also claimed that the AEC could work "near miracles" with nuclear bombs, which was not intellectually honest, because even he acknowledged, in internal documents, significant technical problems with the project.

In Alaska, even businessmen and government officials who favored Project Chariot could not see why Teller wanted a harbor at Cape Thompson because, they reasoned, the harbor would be locked by ice for nine months out of the year. "Teller double-played his interest in performing his experiment and emphasized his inter-est in doing useful public works," writes author O'Neill, because while Teller spoke to the public in Fairbanks, his associates had traveled to Ogotoruk Creek to determine where the bombs would be placed. He had no intention of moving the project elsewhere, and O'Neill contends that Teller knew all along that Project Chariot was an experiment and not a useful public works project. At one point Teller said the AEC could "dig a harbor in the shape of a polar bear if desired." In a classified document, however, Teller wrote that the cratering of dynamics of buried shots in media other than Nevada soil and Pacific coral were "simply not known" and that the Alaska blast would produce useful data "without endangering the Project even if the actual blast was off by 30 percent or more from the calcu-lated size," according to *The Firecracker Boys*.

Author O'Neill also reveals other people who thought some of Tel-ler's associates were somewhat untruthful. A University of Alaska faculty member, Tom English, really challenged two of Teller's asso-ciates about the proposed blast during a meeting on campus in Fairbanks. One was Dr. Harry Kelly, a test-group director in charge of field operations at Livermore, and the other was Dr. Vay Shelton, who came to Alaska to see if they could find some scientist support-ers for Project Chariot. At one of their meetings at the University of Alaska in Fairbanks, according to O'Neill, English said the faculty would not have too much trouble with the men's presentation it if weren't for the AEC's well-known reputation for "mendacity." Keller and Shelton asked for a short break and went to look up the word in the dictionary. When they found out it means "untruthfulness — see synonyms at dishonest," they were furious.

University of Alaska Professor Al Johnson remembers that the fac-ulty "harassed them (the two AEC officials) unmercifully on the sub-ject of fall-out" because faculty members were concerned about the public's being mislead.

Later Johnson himself wrote a letter to the editor to the *Fairbanks Daily News-Miner* about how AEC claimed that "we (Alaskans) have nothing to fear from the amount of radioactive fallout we are receiv-ing or will receive from the various devices." In his letter, however, Johnson goes on to ask, "Are the people of Fairbanks aware that substantially all the geneticists of the world believe that the oppo-site is true? Are they aware that the geneticists can demonstrate that radiation damage produces such conditions as leukemia and bone

tumors in man? Are they aware of the incidence of leukemia in survivors of the Hiroshima blast? I have not encountered this information in the local news media." That's because the AEC was misleading the public and the *Fairbanks Daily News-Miner* was not
questioning these federal officials' "mendacity."

Teller and his associates were not honest with the Alaska people
about Project Chariot. Practically everything Teller told the Alaskan
people, it seemed, was misleading or untruthful. We should all be
glad he never got the chance to complete his original desire to make
a harbor using a 2.4-megaton nuclear detonation in Northwest
Alaska.

Learning about White, Middle-Class America in Rural Alaska

Lucy Nuqarrluk Daniels   *Yup'ik   Elim*

How strange I felt when it dawned on me that my ancestors hadn't
"come over on the *Mayflower*" in 1620. My people had already been
on this continent, living off the land in Alaska for thousands of
years. I realized this only after years of coloring pictures in school
of the Pilgrims in their funny hats every Thanksgiving time.

In my early school years, I mostly felt dumb. For one thing, I had
no concept of miles, let alone inches, feet, and years. I learned how
to use the ruler, all right, but only to draw straight lines. Distance
was usually measured in how long it took to reach a destination by
dog team or boat.

As for north, south, east, and west, well, north was up. South was
down, east was right, and west was left. On a map, that is. I finally
learned where north was as a teenager when my brother pointed it
out to me. That was at Eek (a village by the delta of the Kuskokwim
River). When we moved, I was lost again. I remember sweating over
a set of questions about a map on a standardized achievement test. I
still have no clue as to where NNE is.

And that course in health made very little sense in school. Reading the textbook required pure labor. I had been reading about the
"stone-H" only to discover that it was the stomach.

Every fall, so it seemed, the teacher stressed the merits of brushing one's teeth. One teacher even tried to get us to enter a poster contest on ways of maintaining healthy teeth. We all turned in clean poster paper. At home, I simply picked up a piece of sturdy, dead grass or a sliver of wood and poked food out of my teeth. Every fall, though, I conscientiously brushed my teeth for a week.

I remember in our social studies textbook a group of American students who traveled through South America, learning about the crops each country produced. I wasn't too impressed by how much wheat or flax a certain country grew because I had no idea what wheat and flax were. I only had a rough idea of how long it took Grandma and me to fill a wooden barrel with salmonberries.

When I was almost seventeen, I entered Mt. Edgecumbe High School, a boarding school in southeastern Alaska about a thousand miles from my village. Here was a strange, new world, not only because of the heavy influence of white culture, but also because of its primary population—teenagers.

The strangest course had to be home economics. I could relate to sewing, because Mom had a sewing machine, but cooking was another story. In our first cooking class, we learned how to prepare fresh grapefruit, my first introduction to this fruit. It was strange but okay.

What was not okay was what happened days after we made yeast bread. It started when our teacher said in a smiling voice, "You can tell who mamma's helpers are. Kathy was standing sideways, kneading the dough with one hand while she jabbered away at one of the girls."

Well, I hadn't known how to knead bread dough. Had not my kitchenette mate kneaded it for me, I probably would have flunked that segment of the course. Years later, I realized that I had no need to feel like a failure. You see, Mom had always made sourdough bread. She had shown me that one simply adds two heaping teaspoonfuls—not measuring spoons—of baking soda and enough flour to make thick, heavy dough, then pours the dough into 9-by-13-inch pans and bakes it in a woodstove oven.

At Mt. Edgecumbe, dining room food was also different. My first meal of chicken didn't impress me at all. It tasted so bland that I felt as though I had eaten too much seal oil. What a far cry from moose or duck soup and boiled fish!

I also found English and American literature hard to grasp.

Though I enjoyed the stories and plays, I had trouble analyzing them. I grew up just listening to Grandma's stories. I was already in my teens when I discovered *David Copperfield* and *Treasure Island*. In high school English, I discovered the fascinating world of plays. I enjoyed reading, but I didn't know how to "tear a story apart." And poetry? I never did understand poems, except for "How do I love thee? Let me count the ways." Perhaps. Some of Grandma's stories contained songs, but in a completely different format than sonnets and the like.

I don't know if the school system required us to learn the wrong things. It was just that we entered school ice cold. We had to learn everything from scratch, including our teacher's language. We didn't start school possessing a certain amount of knowledge that a teacher could work with. We had to learn foreign concepts in a foreign language.

Kotzebue

Iñupiaq Educator Provides Link between Elders and Students

Ruthie Sampson   Iñupiaq   Kotzebue

I was born in 1954 and raised in the village of Selawik, Alaska. My earliest memories are of my grandmother, Dora Ballot, whom I affectionately called Aana. I remember her dressing me, packing me on her back, and rowing a small dory on the river as she took me to summer camp.

Living at camp with other families and Elders, I joined a daily routine that included meals with extended family members. We all went on berry-picking trips together, and I played with their children. We did subsistence activities communally, requiring cooperation from everyone.

Growing up in Selawik meant that I knew everyone in the town of just over five hundred people. Every year at Christmas, everyone in the village received a paper bag with his or her name on it, which contained popcorn, hard candy, gum, a few precious mixed nuts, and a cookie or two. Even babies received a bag. As a little girl, I wished that I was a member of the Christmas Candy Committee, because I knew the names of all the adults, children, and babies. At the time, it seemed that the adults could never remember all the names of the babies.

I grew up attending the Selawik Friends Church. I enjoyed going there every Sunday morning and evening as well as on Wednesdays for prayer meetings and on Tuesdays for weekday classes. I had my first bilingual teachers during those weekday classes. They told us Bible stories in both English and Eskimo.

As I attended church over time, I noticed that each year various people were appointed to different positions related to church activities. I learned at an early age that if you were appointed to a job, you were expected to perform your duties without question and without complaint. In fact, all community tasks inside or outside of church followed this code. No one questioned cooperation. We were taught to help one another at an early age. It was "all for one and one for all."

For example, when a person died in the village, everyone helped out according to his or her ability. Certain community members would clean and dress the body while others comforted the family and cooked for the family. Many men would dig the grave. Local talented carpenters would build the coffin and still others would fashion the grave marker. Cooks fed these helpers with food that community members donated. Because helping was always regarded as a reciprocal activity, these helpers did not go unrewarded. During Christmas week, the family of the deceased person would give all the helpers a token gift for their help. These gifts ranged from a simple pair of socks to a beautiful pair of mukluks.

As I lived in the village, I also learned that younger people were expected to help Elders. We were always to respect and listen to their advice. Since I spent so much time with my Aana Dora, I also learned to love the couple who helped raised her: Richard and Fanny Jones. When I was older and more able, I visited this old couple. I would often pack water and carry wood into their house.

I enjoyed sitting beside a certain window located next to their woodstove and just visiting with them. In those days, the evenings in their home would fall still and quiet. Only the gentle hissing of a gasoline lantern and an occasional crackling of the wood stove would accompany the silence. Visiting with this old couple did not require that we talk constantly. This is where I learned to appreciate silence.

Iñupiaq Ruthie Sampson. Kotzebue, Alaska, 1993. Photo by Jim Magdanz.

Secondary education was not available locally when I grew up in Selawik, so I had to move to Anchorage at age fourteen to attend high school. That is when I realized that, although I had attended school for nine years in Selawik, I had never had a chance to study anything about "the Eskimos." When I attended Dimond High School, though, I did learn about Eskimos and other Alaska Natives. I was proud that I could speak the Eskimo language, but I was sad that I had never learned to Eskimo dance. During those years, I also began to think about what I wanted to do after completing school. I became acquainted with an instructor who taught a suicide-prevention class at a local college. As I listened to her lectures, I thought that I should become a social worker. I think I made that decision because of how we were taught to help others.

At age seventeen, I entered the University of Alaska Fairbanks for one year, then transferred to Central Washington State College for another year. During those years, I took sociology courses, but I began to doubt my career decision because the social problems seemed so overwhelming and depressing. Although I felt compelled to help my fellow Eskimos, I wanted to work at a job that was fun and stimulating.

When I was almost nineteen, I returned to Northwest Alaska and worked as a disk jockey at KOTZ, the region's radio station in Kotzebue. As fate would have it, I met my husband, Luke, so I remained in Kotzebue. Then I joined the local Maniilaq Johnson O'Malley Cultural Heritage Program. My job was to work with village researchers who taped Elders.

As I listened to the tapes that had been collected, I became fascinated by all the information that had somehow eluded me when I was growing up. I wondered why I had not learned these things about "the Eskimos" at school. I realized then that Native students should have an opportunity to learn about themselves at school. That year, I helped to produce a bilingual book about traditional Eskimo medicinal practices, titled *Timimun Mamirrutit*.

After that job, I became committed to the idea of transferring the information from our Elders to students in the local school system. I went to work at a national bilingual materials development center in Anchorage for two years to help develop materials for school use. Later, I worked at Sivunigvik, a summer camp in Northwest Alaska that immerses students in Eskimo culture for one week. Then I worked as an Iñupiaq language instructor in Selawik School. Today, I am working as Bilingual Education Coordinator for the Northwest Arctic Borough School District in Kotzebue.

Besides the fact I enjoy my job, I tend to think of my commitment to the Eskimo language and culture as a strong, driving force in my life. Once again, I am able to work with information provided by the Elders. It is a way that I feel I can help other Iñupiaq people. It requires that I be as cooperative as possible. Helping others was instilled in me as a child, and I thank the Lord that I can do my part to contribute to the well-being of the people who live in Northwest Alaska.

Village English Spoken by Young and Old in Rural Alaska

Hannah Paniyavluk Loon   *Iñupiaq*   *Kotzebue*

Village English, a common form of speech in Alaska villages, is a variety of nonstandard English, which educators call a "local English." Here in Northwest Alaska, village English is spoken in most of the communities.

Before western contact, the people spoke the Iñupiaq language in this region. When the early explorers arrived, they not only brought goods to trade, but they came with their language as well. The English language then took hold among the Iñupiat.

After contact, the early missionaries and teachers fanned out in this region. The *naluaġmiu* (white man) established schools and churches with whatever materials were available and in doing so, created permanent villages. Until then, clans of people had lived spread throughout the region at their winter or summer camps.

Unfortunately, when the Iñupiat were taught English in the new schools, they got punished and beaten for speaking their original Native language. As a result, the Iñupiat learned English with much difficulty.

Today, English is the predominant language in this region, yet Iñupiaq still is spoken by a majority of older people. It is rare to hear a child speak fluent Iñupiaq today. A few people in their twenties and thirties speak some Iñupiaq, but mainly English or village English.

Today, it is common to hear people speaking a blend of English and Iñupiaq. If they are not fluent in Iñupiaq, they tend to mix English with incomplete Iñupiaq words or vice versa. In Northwest Alaska, people have gotten used to blending the two languages and have adapted to speaking village English.

For instance, in the office environment, I speak standard English to non-Natives every day, yet I run into situations where I have difficulty explaining typical Native processes, such as how to make a half-dried salmon. Also, I can carry on a conversation in Iñupiaq, especially if I'm comfortable talking to a person. Yet, if I were to explain the process of making a half-dried salmon to a tough guy like Charles Bronson, you would see my mouth open without a single word coming out!

In any case, I can explain or describe a situation to any local person in three different languages: English, village English, and Iñupiaq. I am likely to speak Iñupiaq to an Elder because it is necessary, but I will use village English if someone asks me, for instance, "When you come?" I can quickly switch between village English and standard English. To compare the two languages, in English, a person might say, "I have not eaten yet," whereas in village English, one would say, "I never eat yet." Speakers of village English tend to communicate indirectly rather than directly. For instance, one would say, "Just try taste it," rather than the command, "Taste it."

I do not use proper English with those who speak to me in village English because it may intimidate them or make them feel uncomfortable. For those of us who speak village English, it is best to speak this language only to those who understand it.

Village English exists in me and in many people who live in the communities in Northwest Alaska. Because of my Iñupiaq background, I must admit English is hard to master in speeches and on paper.

Although village English may sound "funny"—meaning "bad"—to English instructors, it has its own beauty to my ears. There's no such thing as "correct" village English. I structure my sentences any way I desire. Rules don't limit village English as long as the listener understands.

Village English is truly a spoken language. It is a form of communication used by the Iñupiaq people of this region, young and old. The Iñupiat generally enjoy the humorous side of life, so they speak village English with a sense of humor. Village English is infectious once you've spent time in the village.

Writer Includes Self
in Definition of Computer Nerd

Calvin "Sonny" Ikkitchiiq Harris   *Iñupiaq*   *Kotzebue*

A computer nerd is a person who is in love with the most frustrating and fascinating piece of plastic, metal, and glass ever invented. Some people think of a computer as a fancy typewriter that doesn't need White Out. Being something of a computer nerd, I know there is another side to the story.

Once upon a time I applied for a job as an assistant planner at Maniilaq Association, a nonprofit social service organization, in Kotzebue. I was hired! I felt wonderful! Then worry set in. Being computer illiterate, I was afraid I wouldn't be able to do the work involved. I did simple tasks at the beginning. Then I was introduced to IBM personal computers. It was love at first byte.

Maniilaq's planner decided that I should get some training in DOS, the Disk Operating System for IBM computers. I went to Fairbanks for that training. Then to support Maniilaq's comprehensive planning system, we ordered a Mac SE/30 and *MacProject* (project management software).

By then, I liked computers so much that I started to do something unusual in our organization. I started playing with computers. This confirmed my growing status as a computer nerd. I would do things like take *command.com* out of the "C" directory to see what would happen. Well, if you take *command.com* out, you can't restart your computer from the hard disk. You have to use a floppy disk to reinstall *command.com.* Not knowing that, I had to call our technical adviser in Anchorage to troubleshoot the mess I'd made. I was dreading that call. He let me know in no uncertain terms that he was annoyed.

"That's what you get when you play with your computer!" he said sternly.

But that didn't stop me. I kept playing with computers. Once a computer nerd, always a computer nerd.

Iñupiaq Sonny Harris.
Kotzebue, Alaska, 1992.
Photo by Jim Magdanz.

•Kotzebue

Because many Maniilaq staff were afraid of their computers, I wanted to show them that computers were understandable. People started asking me to troubleshoot problems with their computers, then printer difficulties. Being a nerd, I liked fixing computers and peripherals. I would gladly look at anything remotely connected to computers. Soon I was being asked to install various kinds of software on Maniilaq computers, to set up files needed to manage programs, and to train users on their PCs. I was always stretching to learn about the software so I could teach others.

Nerds know computers are incredibly versatile. You can get a computer to calculate problems that would take days to figure out by hand. You can edit memos and letters just by cutting and pasting. You can create art and music. You can chat with other computer users, call up libraries, and even read a newspaper from Anchorage. All you need is a computer, accompanying software, a modem, and the will to experiment.

After I had taught myself most of what I needed to know at work, my supervisor and I started thinking that I should get more formal training. I started with training in Anchorage on the System/36, a minicomputer used for accounting, payroll, and word-processing. Later, I went for training in Seattle for a course called Hardware Maintenance and Repair, which applied to microcomputers such as the IBM PS/2 and PC XT. Again, that was only a taste of what could be learned in the field.

I have learned that about 95 percent of computer problems are people-oriented (such as pressing the wrong key). The other 5 percent of problems are usually due to loose cabling and internal malfunctions.

After a while, people whom I had helped saw I knew what I was doing. One day the health education staff made me a certificate (Computer Whiz-Kid Award) which I keep on my door. I'm proud of it, I like it, and I don't think I'll ever take it down.

Higher Education in Northwest Alaska: A Dream Realized

Berda Willson   Iñupiaq   Nome

I consider education a precious gift that should not be taken for granted, especially in rural Alaska, where formal education can require exceptional efforts to obtain. In 1944, when I was four, my family and I were living in the village of Nuuk, a very small fish camp about twenty miles east of Nome in Northwest Alaska. That year, my dad had decided that my older sister and two older brothers would attend school in Nome. As the youngest, I wasn't old enough to enroll.

Unfortunately, a devastating diphtheria epidemic had erupted throughout Nome in 1944, and three of us children contracted this dreaded disease. Although rare in today's modern world because of immunization, diphtheria can be fatal without the administration of an antitoxin. Of the forty-five known cases in Nome that year, two people died, according to articles in 1944 issues of the *Nome Nugget* newspaper. The first to die was my cousin, the only daughter of my Aunt Margaret. My father, while grieving his niece's death, felt most anxious to leave Nome for the safety of his own children. Finally well enough to travel and considering ourselves fortunate to be alive, we all moved back to Nuuk for the winter. My dad, furious about the danger his family was placed in, vowed at the time never to move the family to Nome again. According to my dad, my eight-year-old brother, Glen, who almost died, took two years to fully recover. School, at least for that year, was forgotten.

Three years passed before the family again moved to Nome for school, where my brother and I started first grade together. Glen was nine, I was seven. Despite our "advanced" age, we did not feel out of place, because some children in our first-grade class were as old as twelve. In those days, several age groups commonly clustered into one class. Many students attended school irregularly, especially if, like our family, they lived off the land within a subsistence way of life.

My siblings and I always started school at least six weeks late each fall. We also left six weeks early each spring, if we managed to attend at all. My dad carved ivory in the winter, but our main livelihood was fishing. We typically sold just enough fish each summer to buy staples to supplement our diet of mainly fish. Hard times in Nome in the 1940s and '50s meant that if you did not put up fish, meat, and berries in the summer and into the fall, you could go hungry over the long winter. Survival meant working constantly not only to keep all our stomachs full, but to stay warm, because wood was our fuel for both heating and cooking.

Life was hard. At times, we children rebelled against the never-ending chores. Summer chores for my brothers meant hauling water from the well, getting wood and chopping it for winter, tending the fish nets, and in general, doing "boy" work to help my dad. Winter chores were a little easier. My brothers hauled snow for water and chopped kindling. Of course, in winter there was school. My sister and I baked bread, cooked, washed dishes, and did other household chores all year. When we had visitors, in order not to keep "company" waiting for a clean dish or something to eat, my brothers had to help wash dishes and do household chores. We all had to pick berries and help cut fish for smoking, salting, pickling, and drying during the short summer season.

One fall, after high water made our well salty, my brother Mel ran away rather than continue to pump the well to make it fresh again. He returned after a few days, and life continued on, difficult as ever. Through it all, though, we still hungered for a formal education.

I especially dreamed of a college education, even as I struggled to keep up in elementary school in Nome, despite sporadic attendance. Thankfully, our dad taught us at home whenever we could not afford to move to Nome to attend school. My sister, Marie, did not finish high school and married young. My brothers both joined the Air Force before completing high school. Many years later, however, they took exams and received their General Educational Development diplomas. For my part, I decided to persevere, intending to graduate from high school with an eye ever focused on a college degree.

Unfortunately, I was just starting my senior year in 1957 at Nome

High School when my college dream vanished with my dad's death. An old man at age seventy-two, Dad died of a stroke complicated by pneumonia. My father had worked long and hard during his later years of life to raise his young family as a single parent, even when we children did not fully appreciate it. He had never given up on us. If he had lived, my father would have continued carving ivory and scrimping together funds to put me through college. At the time of his death, however, I was working a part-time job for $1.50 an hour. It just wasn't enough.

Scholarships and other financial support for potential college students like me hardly existed in the 1950s, and especially not for Native women living in rural Alaska. In addition, Nome would have no local college until many years later. No one had ever heard of "audioconference" or "distance delivery" classes in the 1950s. At that time, rural Alaskans had to be able to move to Fairbanks, Sitka, or even the Lower 48 to attend college. Very few, including me, could afford such expense. In the 1950s and 1960s, a woman in rural Alaska, particularly a Native woman, was expected to marry, raise a family, and depend on her husband. Since educational opportunities, especially beyond high school, were virtually nonexistent, I took the "easy" way out. I married young, even graduating from high school as a married woman.

I worked for many years as a homemaker, raising a family of four boys and one girl, all the while keeping my dream of attending college alive. When Northwest Community College opened its doors in Nome in the early 1970s, I eagerly began taking classes. Unfortunately, I did not enjoy in my previous marriage the support that I have today with my present husband to attend the local college regularly. Consequently, not until the early 1980s, after I remarried, did I begin to vigorously pursue college classes again. By 1986, I had earned a Certificate in Business from Northwest Community College, then continued on for an associate's degree.

As I inched along toward my two-year associate's degree, I also was juggling a full-time job, family responsibilities, classes, homework, and housework. During this time, I also served on the board of directors for Council Native Corporation, as treasurer, which required keeping its books and attending regular meetings. My work as office manager at the local utilities company meant attending several evening meetings a month. I tried to "do it all." Unfortunately, in January 1989, I became very ill with an allergic reaction that caused my liver to stop functioning for several days. My education dream again faded as I struggled at first against death, then to regain my health.

As I grew stronger, I thought of college again. I cautiously enrolled in classes again. Since I had been so ill that I almost died, I asked myself, "Why am I doing this? Couldn't I be doing something else that perhaps would make me happier, even just momentarily, than to attend such grueling college classes?" As I thought about it more, though, slowly the answer was revealed to me: I desperately wanted a college degree. Sheer persistence kept me going until May 1990, when at age fifty, I graduated with an Associate of Applied Science degree with a major in business.

My wonderful husband, Steve, has proudly attended my graduation ceremonies. Without his untiring support, I would have failed and probably dropped out. This man has cooked, cleaned house, and performed any other chore, no matter how menial, to help me achieve my goal. Other family members such as my sons and daughter-in-law have helped, too, by doing dishes and cleaning house for me. My only daughter, Melissa, who has been attending Northwest College simultaneously, has lent support, too. She has tutored me (her math was fresher than mine). She has criticized my work with a daughter's honesty, telling me when a paper was, frankly, "Just awful, Mom." Then she would suggest ways to improve it. At times Melissa became my mentor. Both she and my husband, Steve, believed I could succeed. They offered the courage to persevere when I wanted to quit.

Despite achieving my two-year degree, I still had not satisfied my hunger for higher education. I plowed right on toward a bachelor's degree in Rural Development at Northwest College, which by the late 1980s had become a branch campus of the University of Alaska Fairbanks. However, this time I am wiser. I have learned to pace myself. I am a lot more organized. Before I sign up for a class, for example, I call the instructor and ask about course requirements so I won't get overloaded. I also try to take similar classes together in order to complement course content. I am honest with myself and with my instructors. If I can't complete an assignment on time, I let them know and complete it as soon as I can. If I fall behind, I don't berate myself. I just reschedule my work and continue.

I cannot let my dream die. I want the personal satisfaction of earning a bachelor of arts degree. If I can keep up the pace, I will graduate at the end of spring semester 1996, at age fifty-six, along with my daughter, who is a candidate for the same degree. My dream will be realized. I hope that by fulfilling it I can motivate others to continue with their educational goals in rural Alaska. I feel that education is the answer for Alaska Natives to meet the challenge of living in two worlds. It is also my sincere hope that I have served as a role model for my daughter and will serve as a role model in education for other Native women, young and old.

My road to higher education has been long, tedious, and sometimes agonizing due to illness and other choices I had made earlier in life. Nevertheless, I have made it this far and don't intend to give up now. I feel most fortunate to attend college in Nome. If I did not have the local educational opportunities, I would not have realized my lifelong dream.

Tears sting my eyes when I think about receiving that diploma at graduation. I know I will be so proud of my daughter, Melissa, but I also will be thinking of that little girl in Nuuk who finally became a college graduate at an age when other folks are thinking about retirement.

Berda Willson completed her B.A. in Rural Development through the University of Alaska Fairbanks College of Rural Alaska in May 1996.

5

Traditional and Western Cultures

Since civilization has swept into their lives in tide-like earnestness,
it has left the Eskimos, Indians, and Aleuts in a bewildering state
of indecision and insecurity between the seeming need for assimila-
tion, and the desire to retain some of their cultural and traditional
way of life. — HOWARD ROCK, Iñupiaq, October 1962

Throughout the world, indigenous cultures have experienced dramatic, often violent change in their way of life after outside cultures
arrived. The same is true in Alaska; nevertheless, in the face of injus-
tice, remarkable triumphs of adaptability and survival often arise.

For instance, Blanche Jones Criss writes about how she and her
brother coped with the clash between Native and Christian spirituality that endures into modern times, when missionaries arrived in
her village "carrying Bibles." Or, Rena Boolowon Booshu discusses
how young people today choose whom they want to marry while
holding on to some of the practices of a traditional Siberian Yup'ik
marriage. Julia Stalker first experiences Eskimo dancing as an adult.
Eva Menadelook, writing shortly before the fall of the Soviet empire,
longs for the time when her island village of Little Diomede traded
freely across the border with Russian relatives in the Bering Sea.
Lucy Daniels recalls how Yup'ik people traditionally dealt with death
and reflects on some positive changes in how people grieve.

Many people, including many Alaskans, do not realize that legal
segregation was practiced in Alaska against Natives during territorial days. Yup'ik Karla Rogers tells about it in her award-winning essay about the brave young Native woman who is the Rosa Parks of
Alaska history.

Both Iñupiaq Charlene Ferguson and Yup'ik Spencer Rearden
write about what it means to be an Alaska Native by reflecting on
their own experiences.

Athabascan Becky Gallen offers a lesson for all of us about over-
coming the legacy of destruction inherited by adult children of alcoholics. Likewise, Geri Reich reaches beyond herself when she tells

about discovering on the streets of Anchorage a close friend trapped in a cycle of alcohol; she paid his airfare home to Kotzebue, where he began trying to put his life back together.

High school senior Verné Seum writes with poignant insight about the clash of generations in her own family that affects so many peoples around the world. Alaska Native people who have read this essay consider it a superb crystallization of the painful dilemma that Native people face in modern times.

Finally, this final section of the book shows that modern-day Alaska Natives face many of the same problems that families throughout America are facing: how to earn a decent living while being responsible, nurturing parents who are "there"—spiritually, culturally, and physically—for their children. In this context consider Geri Reich's heart-rending and confusing separation from her children and hometown Kotzebue while pursuing her career as a tradesperson at the Red Dog Mine. On the other hand, young people also are learning to "be there" for their parents by helping out with household chores and adapting to homes where there is a single parent or where both parents work outside the home, as revealed in Tony Lincoln's selection.

Alaska Natives traditionally were a nomadic people who traveled with the seasons as they followed the fish and game. Despite the tremendous challenges in assimilating dramatic cultural changes, this chapter speaks to the extraordinary adaptability, perseverance, and resilience of Alaska's first people, along with their enduring reverence for tradition.

When People Carrying Bibles Came

Blanche Jones "B. J." Criss   Iñupiaq   Kotzebue

In the early twentieth century, missionaries introduced Western religion to the Native Iñupiaq Eskimos of Northwest Alaska, which changed Native Iñupiaq beliefs from traditional shamanism to Christianity.

My great-grandparents were the first generation introduced to the Quakers, who were the founders of the Friends Church in Northwest Alaska.

As a small child, I listened to my great-grandparents tell stories of how thankful they were that these "people who look different" came. My great-grandparents told of spirits whispering in the air at dusk and of how they had to dance until these shamanistic spirits went away. When these people carrying Bibles came, my great-grandparents were happy because they made these evil spirits go away.

My mother, as a member of another generation belonging to this new religion, took to the missionaries' ways with great faith by following her leaders. In yet another generation, I found myself in the middle of a vigorous transition period for religion in my hometown of Kotzebue.

For example, during this time, we as members of this religion were not allowed many of the fun things that others did, such as going to local dances, including the local Eskimo dance festivities. We could not go to the movies, either. We also weren't allowed to listen to pop music in our home in Kotzebue, and, among other things, we could not play cards or read comic books.

I left Kotzebue to attend boarding school at the Wrangell Institute in Southeast Alaska during high school, where I was introduced to many of these once-forbidden activities. In boarding school, dancing and pop music were considered recreational pastimes, not something evil, and I enjoyed them very much.

I also learned that this school's main focus was not religion, as had been the case at home in Kotzebue. Part of me felt I should not pursue many of these school activities. Consequently, I found myself with mixed feelings while taking part anyway.

Each spring, after being gone all year, my family and I would excitedly share bits and pieces of news and adventure. Because we were still in the middle of this religious transition, however, I left out many stories of fun events away from home. That made me feel shame and loneliness. Ironically, it was the same loneliness I experienced while away at school, so far from home.

My mother, following her leaders and condemning my actions, made me feel hate and rebellion toward our religion. My brother, Frank, being more of an activist, and who also went to boarding school, would argue these issues fervently with whoever would listen.

For example, Frank challenged the fact that the *Sunday Pix*, a comic-book-style reader that the church handed out to the class during Sunday School, resembled the regular kind of comic book that kids liked to read. He pointed out that the comic book is like an animated movie with no motion, except that we read the words rather than listen to the voices. Frank never felt as if he received an adequate answer to these kinds of discrepancies, which he felt were valid and legitimate issues for discussion.

Frank, whom I called "the great philosopher," raised many good issues during this time that I believe were never fully answered. For example, I don't believe he ever received what he would consider a valid answer for why, as Friends Church members, we cannot Eskimo dance.

Yet, despite the problems and family disruptions the new religion caused, I still applaud these people with Bibles who paved their way into Northwest Alaska. Through strict discipline, they showed the Native Iñupiat Christian ways and taught them the English language. These things have linked the Iñupiat to the Western world.

After a century of regrouping and reorganizing, I have a sense that the next generation will have stronger faith and values to pass on to their children. With the Friends Church members' blessings, perhaps succeeding generations will participate in Eskimo dance festivities.

A unique part of history has taken place within my lifetime. For that I am proud.

Death, a Part of Life

Lucy Nuqarrluk Daniels   *Yup'ik*   *Elim*

As a member of the Yup'ik Eskimo community, I was brought up to accept death as a part of life. From early childhood, I participated in certain customs and observed attitudes regarding death. Only now have I begun to unearth the meaning behind the customs and attitudes with the help of my parents, Calvin and Sophie Coolidge of Nunapitchuk, and information from the Rasmuson Library at the University of Alaska Fairbanks.

My first memory of death is from when I was about eight years old. There was an old man in the village who seemed to cough incessantly. One night, I thought I heard him walking back and forth by our house, coughing. The next day, Grandma told me that he had died.

"Yuunrirtuq," she said, or "He/She is no longer a person." Grandma took me along to see the widow, my grandmother's good friend. When we entered the home the couple had shared, a mud-roofed log house, people from the village had already gathered to sit with the grieving family. We found our places on the floor next to a wall and just sat quietly. On a mat on the floor in the middle of the one-room house lay the body of the old man.

In subsequent years, I participated in many such gatherings. My father told me he does not know the meaning behind this practice of sitting with the grieving family. He only knows that it's a way of being with the "ones left behind," helping where they need help, and trying to keep them happy. Usually, the body of the person who had died was kept in the home for two days before it was moved to the church. During that time, various people from the village stayed with the family, both day and night.

About two years after my first awareness of death, I remember lying next to Grandma in our family tent at fish camp when we began to hear a commotion outside.

"Something must have happened to Aataurluq," Grandma said,

meaning "poor, dear father," the name we called the old man who lived next door to us.

"Why don't you wait here while I check on Aataurluq," she suggested to me. We called the old man's wife "poor, dear mother."

When I refused to stay behind, Grandma took me along. When we entered the old couple's tent, Grandma went to sit next to the old woman, her dear friend. I slid onto the log by the tent door, one of four logs that lie at the base of the floorless, white, canvas tent.

At the right back corner, on his cot, lay the old man, breathing heavily. My father and another man were tending to him.

"Perhaps, if we turn his head this way," said one man.

They turned his head to one side, but the old man started breathing noisily, as though snoring. They turned his head to its original position. The other man must have asked Dad to pray, because he removed his cap, and holding it in both hands in front of him, bowed his head in prayer. Shortly thereafter, the old man stopped breathing. One man filled a basin with plain water and washed the old man's body with a cloth.

The old couple's daughter-in-law, who was married to the older of the two sons, was sent twice to summon her husband. Each time she returned alone. The second time, she said her husband's heart was bothering him. Periodically, the old woman wiped her tears with her fingers but remained calm.

Someone must have been sent for the younger son from the family's home village, about a ten-minute boat ride away, because he stomped through the entrance, with another man right behind him.

"What happened?" the son demanded.

"He was taking a steam bath," said one man. "When he delayed coming out, we checked on him and found him."

"We never let him take steam baths alone," said the son's companion. "When we do, we watch him closely."

Turning to his mother, the son ordered, "You, go out."

"That, I will not do," the old woman answered quietly, using an expression of disbelief in Eskimo.

Since this incident, I have learned that the practice of washing the dead person's body is a recent one. My parents both told a story about a woman from the Dillingham area who was reported to have gotten up and out of her coffin after the funeral was over. According to the story, the woman said that Jesus had told her to return and

wash herself. After she washed and fixed herself up, the woman lay
down in her coffin and "no longer had breath," or *anernerirluni*, as
Dad put it.

My parents also described various taboos connected with death.
For example, Mom told me that her first awareness of these taboos
occurred when her grandmother, her father's mother, had died. She
explained that Grandpa had said something about "after these five
days had passed" that he would again be able to "do things."

Dad said the number of "taboo days" was five for a deceased man
and four for a deceased woman. In these days, said Dad, the relatives "left behind" were to avoid using a sharp implement or going
out for the purpose of hunting, trapping, getting wood, or doing
other activities outside the village.

Dad said violations of the taboos caused food sources, such as
fish, to suddenly become unavailable. According to Mom, the relatives of the one who died were warned not to chop with an ax or to
cut with an *uluaq*, or woman's knife, so that the one who died
would not be kept from moving forward or onward. Should this occur, that person could start appearing or causing strange happenings to scare the living. Mom said that the people believed that if
the one who died lost his or her way, he or she might wander aim-
lessly in the afterlife.

Mom also said she became aware of another taboo when she visited a woman who had lost her adopted son. The bereaved mother
told Mom that though she wished to sew, she was refraining, because she and others had been warned not to sew in the evenings
after a relative had died. Mom said women were told not to sew in
the evenings because, by pulling the thread, they might pull the
dead person back. Mom said the women probably feared they might
witness strange happenings if they disregarded the taboo.

When I started participating in the customs surrounding death, I
heard older women admonishing younger women to "try to be
good," especially when the latter had trouble controlling their grief.
In one village, I went to a young couple's home just hours after their
infant son had died. The baby had been placed on a mat on top of a
box, I believe. At one point, the mother started weeping audibly.

"Try to be good," an older women said consolingly. "It's better to
try to be good."

Mom said all were told not to cry too excessively for the one who
had died, for those who do, wet that one with their tears and nasal

mucus, making him or her suffer, as though he or she were wallowing in a slimy substance.

Mom told a story about a "poor woman" who always cried after her child had died. Another woman told her that she had seen the woman's child in a dream. In that dream, the child was unable to be happy. The child appeared to be in a "slimy substance," the hair dripping with the stuff. Mom said, if she remembered correctly, the deceased child told the woman to tell the mother that he or she was weary of suffering in water and mucus.

Talking with my parents, I discovered that, unlike the people of old, I grew up with the notion that people went somewhere else after they died. Dad said only the *angalkuut*, or shamans, were said to go to the *ircenrraat* at death when the ircenrraat used to "bring (people) in." Dad said the ircenrraat lived underground or had entrances on the bluffs of hills. Before the people were "brought in," it would get so foggy they were unable to see anything. Only after they were "brought in" would it clear up.

In the ircenrraat domain, those who were "brought in" recognized the angalkuut who had died, now living. Dad said the people who were taken underground always found themselves in the *ircenrraat qasgiq* or the men's "communal house." When the time came for the "brought in" to leave, they saw three doors, one on top of the other. They were told not to do anything else but to just exit through the middle door. If they did so, they reached home. If they went through the bottom door, they found themselves underground. Exit through the top door, and they ended up in midair.

Both Mom and Dad said that the people of old acted as though the ones who had died were still living among them. Mom said at Qaariitaaq, the time when the children went from house to house wearing masks, her father used to pretend that his mother was among them. Dad said the people pretended that those who had died were still alive and believed that they still used their possessions, and that was why their belongings were placed around their coffins.

"I used to see kayaks, even sleds (by the coffins)," Dad said. In those days, said Dad, the dead were placed in boxes made of logs and situated on logs on top of the ground.

Growing up in a Yup'ik Eskimo community, I gradually became aware of the custom of a grieving family always giving a feast after the burial of a loved one.

My father did not know the meaning behind this custom when I asked him, but a paper from the Rasmuson Library of the University of Alaska Fairbanks may shed light on the origin of this traditional feast. In a Lower Kuskokwim School District publication titled, "Yup'ik Lore: Oral Traditions of an Eskimo People," Ells Lewis of Bethel describes how local villagers gave delectable food to the one who had died and tells how this food was distributed to the people after the burial.

When Grandma died in the 1970s, I flew home from Fairbanks, where I was attending the University of Alaska. After I reached Bethel, my brother chartered an air taxi, and he and I and his four children flew on to Eek, my folks' home village at that time.

When we arrived, Dad told me, "Take the children next door to see "Aanaq" meaning "mother," the name we called Grandma, who had already been placed in the church. When my brother took the children, I went along. Not until the villagers filed up the aisle to view Grandma's body did Grandma's death become real to me.

When I had seen Grandma on my way to Fairbanks in August, she had told me, "This is probably the last time we're seeing each other." I had been a bit puzzled then, but her words became reality.

Grandma had been more than just a grandmother. She had been like a second mother to me. When I was a girl, she took me everywhere with her. When I became a teenager, she transferred that caring to my little sister, who was also at the funeral.

My mother, her daughter-in-law, had taken Grandma in. She had lived with us ever since I could remember. In her last days when Grandma was too weak to care for herself, Mom had been her care giver. There, as the villagers said good-bye to Grandma, my mom, my sister, and I wept openly.

During the burial, my sister and I prepared for the feast at our folks' home. While we were serving those who had come to share our grief, I felt release from the pain I had felt during the funeral.

Another tradition related to death is the giving of names. Growing up, I noticed that one woman was endeared to me. Grandma used to give this woman the portion of the fall grass I had cut for mukluk insoles. I called her Aipaq, meaning "companion." Not until I was older did I understand that "Aipaq" had been pals with my father's sister who had died and whom I had been named after. That's how she got to be Aipaq.

According to Dad, people named their children after those who had died to try to help the bereaved family. The bereaved person or family treated these children as though they were the relatives who had died.

A woman in one village told me that after her brother died, she was unable to get over her sadness for her brother. One day she prepared special food and took it to the child who had been named after her brother. Only then did she feel better.

Shortly after my cousin died, my nephew was named after him. When my older brother and his wife took their baby boy (my nephew) to see my aunt and her husband, I went along. My aunt and her husband met my brother and his wife at the door. As my sister-in-law handed the baby to my aunt, my aunt cradled the baby in her arms. As she and her husband walked toward the bedroom, my aunt looked into the baby's face and said, "Waniwaurluq" or "here is the poor, dear one."

Death is a part of life. Human beings of any culture are deeply hurt when it occurs. The Yup'ik Eskimo community has found ways to deal with death as a society. Though some of the customs have lost their original meaning, they enhance healing by emphasizing life.

However, admonitions such as "try to be good" or "strong" hurt more than they help, perhaps. Of late, subjects such as death and dying and the grieving process have begun to be discussed more openly, which gives the grieving person the freedom to talk about his or her feelings without censorship. To me, this trend was expressed by an Elder Yup'ik leader, who has since died, when he commented, "We know now that we are not to try to be too strong." This he said when he and his good friend were talking about a younger fellow Yup'ik leader who was killed in a plane crash.

I, myself, found this openness to talk about the process of grieving helpful.

Eskimo Dance: A Tradition of My People

Julia Jones Anausuk Stalker   Iñupiaq   Kotzebue

When I was growing up in the 1960s at Selawik in Northwest Alaska, I never had heard of Eskimo dancing. Then, in 1975 after our parents moved to Kotzebue, we saw Eskimo dancing for the first time during the annual Fourth of July Trade Fair celebration.

In the old days, my parents didn't teach us Eskimo dancing because it was forbidden by the Christian missionaries. I guess we were too young to understand what Eskimo dancing really meant and why the people danced on special occasions. Today, though, I am learning the history of my people's traditional dance rituals.

Recently, my mother explained to me that Eskimo dancing has been passed on from generation to generation. Today, some families join a group—for instance, in Kotzebue, the Northern Lights Dancers—to practice and to learn how to dance. Dancers wear traditional clothing and sing traditional songs, but the people no longer practice the tradition of shamanism in their Eskimo dancing.

"Long ago, our forefathers lived under the rules of a shaman, because there were no other ways to communicate with the other villages," my mother, Ella Avilluqtaq Jones, told me. "The shaman would stand in the center of the group and dance. They met in a little hut called a *hathgi*. In those days, there were no doctors, so the people depended on the shamans to heal the sick."

My mother was told that long ago when the Christian missionaries arrived, they learned that the shaman got his power from dancing to the unknown spirits, and that the missionaries said those "unknown spirits" were considered evil. So the missionaries put a stop to Eskimo dancing because it was against their Christian religion. Instead of dancing to the unknown spirits, the people were taught to attend the Friends Church on a regular basis.

According to Dinah and David Frankson's book, *Whaling: A Way of Life*, Eskimo dancing was also a way of celebrating life along the coast of Alaska, such as in the village of Point Hope. Long ago, the Eskimos danced under the "new moon," encouraging the young single men to dance. Each male danced around a chosen lady and kissed her. If he was successful with her, the young man chose her to be his wife.

They danced until the last person left the dance area. To end the first or second night, they would dance again, but this time the dance meant something more: to let the spirits go "who have roamed around the village."

The ancient ritual of dance is stated this way in an encyclopedia: "Early cultures believed through dancing they could communicate with the unseen spirit world, which controlled the visible world." Today, Eskimo dancers from Alaska and Russia travel to faraway places to perform in celebration. It does seem as though they unite in one spirit.

In 1992, my husband and I joined a whaling crew whose captain was called Towksjeas. We were whaling off the Arctic coast near Point Hope, and our crew had landed a bowhead whale. My husband and I had the privilege to join in Eskimo dancing for the first time in our lives. We were following the ancient Iñupiat tradition that if your crew is successful in the hunt, you dress up in traditional ceremonial clothes and dance with the rest of the crew in celebration.

This dance took place at Point Hope when we were celebrating the catch of the whale. It felt scary to go out and dance in front of the people, especially when it was my first time. I dared myself to go out there. I thought I would make mistakes until I actually joined in the dancing. There, all I did was follow along with the other women. When the song was over, we laughed together.

I can now say that I dance the Eskimo way.

Families Help Define
the Meaning of "Native"

Spencer Rearden   *Yup'ik*   *Kotzebue*

Everyone probably has an idea of what a "Native" is. The legal definition in the Alaska Native Claims Settlement Act says that in order to be Native, a person has to have a certain percentage of Eskimo, Indian, or Aleut blood. My definition is based more on what people do and what is important in their everyday life, such as their belief in tradition and culture. I think that "family" defines much of what Native means. Native people are what they are because of their families and what their families teach them.

Most villages in Alaska consist of many Native families that are related to one another. For instance, in Kotlik, my mother's home village, about five hundred people reside there, and twenty-one closely related families make up the community.

In a village, in the spirit of one big family, everybody takes care of one another. Families share food. Animals caught are shared throughout the village. Native cultural values say that if a person shares, that person will catch more animals in the future. For instance, when I visited Kotlik, I went hunting for beluga whales. The two boats used for the hunt held many people, most of them related. The person who first harpooned the whale got the honor of taking any part of the whale he wanted. Each person who hunted the whale picked out what he wanted, and when we returned to the village, we awarded much of the blubber and meat to other families.

Not only is sharing important, but the activities surrounding food gathering also play an important role in being Native. Entire families pick salmonberries together in the fall. My mom usually does most of the berry picking in our family because she enjoys it, but living in Kotzebue, salmonberries are harder to find. So when I visited Bethel for a summer, I picked salmonberries with my friend Henry and his family. Henry's family knew that we might not get any salmonberries for the winter, so they helped pick berries for us. I remember seeing a carpet of orange salmonberries on the miles of flat tundra. To make picking faster and more entertaining, Henry's brothers, sisters, and I had a race to see who could pick the most berries. Families make up an important part of the subsistence gathering efforts.

Families also help keep traditions alive. The older generations in a family are needed to pass on traditions to younger generations. Just as my grandmother taught my mother how to do traditional activities, my mother teaches us how to do traditional activities. For instance, when I killed my first seal, my mother taught me to give it water. It is believed that the seal's spirit will live on if one gives it fresh water. I gave all of the seal to the Elders so that I could have many more successful hunts in the future. This knowledge and my actions make me Native.

Spiritual activities in many villages revolve around families. Yup'ik villages have annual potlatches. Families celebrate their children's first dances or a relative's first kill of an animal.

When I experienced my first potlatch, everybody brought food. Most of it included traditional Eskimo food. People come from other villages to celebrate a potlatch. Potlatches bring families together and keep them close. Also it teaches the important Native traditions of being generous and showing appreciation for a young person's graduation into adulthood.

Gambell

Components of a Traditional Siberian Yup'ik Marriage

Rena Boolowon Booshu   *Siberian Yup'ik   Gambell*

In a traditional Siberian Yup'ik marriage, couples did not fall in love and then decide whether to get married, as we do today.

In a traditional Siberian Yup'ik marriage, the man was allowed to choose whom he wanted to marry. The female could not choose. If a man could not find a partner, or if a woman wasn't asked, their parents decided who they would marry. Also, females were asked for marriage only after they had their first menstrual period.

Traditional marriages consisted of five steps. The first step is called *aghnangllaq*. The literal translation of this is to "make a woman," which meant that the man's oldest relative, from the father's side, would ask the woman's parents if their daughter could marry.

If the parents agreed, then she would be considered "marked," so that no one else could ask her to marry. The rough translation for "marked" is *tuusimaat*, but translated literally, it means the woman was "stepped all over" by her future parents-in-law! This second step is called *tuunniiq*.

At times, tuunniiq could come before aghnangllaq. For example, if a boy wanted to marry a girl but she was not yet ready, he would ask for her to be marked or "stepped on" first.

As for the third step, *tukfightuq*, if the woman's immediate family accepted the proposal, the man's family then gathered together traditional food, hunting equipment, and kitchen utensils; skins from seals, foxes, reindeer, and polar bears; as well as other things from relatives to "buy" the woman. Two sled loads were usually considered enough, but sometimes one sled was acceptable, too.

Nengawiga is the fourth step in which the man works for the woman's parents. He labored one to four years, depending on how long her father thought his daughter was "worth." If her father was fair, the man was lucky enough to work for only one year.

Although there were five steps to getting married, the couple was considered "married" by the fourth step, because usually they would have started a family by then. During the nengawiga period, the man would sneak over to the woman during the night and sleep with her. She might have tried to run away from the man at first, but she would give in to him in the end. This is called *getgeghaataq*. Sometimes getgeghaataq even happened before the nengawiga, or the fourth stage.

The fifth and last step was called *ukughhita*. The woman's family would collect sled loads of equipment, just as the man's side did earlier, and would present the equipment to the couple for their use. Then the woman's parents would chaperone the new couple over to the man's family's house, where they would now live.

Among the other traditions people practiced were these: One, if the husband mistreated his wife, her father would take her back. Two, when the couple bore children, they were offered gifts. Three, if a man were to get a woman pregnant without asking her parents to marry her, he was held responsible by having to automatically marry her.

Today, our traditions have changed. For example, the tuunniiq and ukughhita steps aren't practiced most of the time. In the nengawiga step, the woman's father lets her husband work for only a year or less. Also, the newlywed couple can live by themselves instead of staying at the man's parents' household. At times, couples also will sleep with each other without being prepared for marriage.

Although Siberian Yup'iks still practice some traditional steps today, young people ultimately decide who will be their mate and if they want to spend the rest of their lives together. Like other young people across America, we Siberians decide whom we want to marry.

Growing Up in the Shadow of the Ice Curtain

Eva Menadelook   Iñupiaq   *Little Diomede*

• Little Diomede

My great-grandfather, Yalaali, fled from his village, Inchoan, in the Russian Far East, about a hundred years ago.

As a young man, he used to roam the land and hunt game for long stretches of time. But one time, soon after his return from a journey, an epidemic swept through the village. Many people died. The village became outraged and planned to execute him because they thought he was responsible. To save his life, Yalaali's family urged him to flee.

He fled to Naukak, also in the Soviet Far East (now called the Settlement of Naukan), where he stayed until he heard that his executioners were coming; then he escaped across the Chukchi sea ice to Big and Little Diomede Islands.

He married a woman from Little Diomede and bore two children, a son and a daughter. This is all we know about our great-grandfather. Had the Ice Curtain between the United States and the Soviet Union remained open after 1947, we would have known more about our Siberian relatives, their genealogy, and their history.

When the border closed, many of the villagers on Little Diomede on the U.S. side fell between the ages of five and ten. When the grandparents of these children died, information about Siberian genealogy and family history died with them. This created a generation that knows little of its Siberian genealogy and family history. The closing of the border froze all other information between families of Little Diomede and relatives in the Chukotka region on the Soviet side.

After the border closed, little contact was possible over the years between Alaskan and Siberian relatives. Occasionally, a Chukchi Siberian skin boat would voyage to the international dateline located between Big and Little Diomede. The villagers from Little Diomede would meet the skin boat to exchange news of relatives. But even letters could not be easily transferred between the two islands.

The closing of the border affected all the villagers of Little Diomede. For instance, in July 1947, a group of nineteen Natives from the village voyaged to Chukotka. On that same day, the U.S. Department of Interior sent word to the Bureau of Indian Affairs schoolteacher in the village stating that the border was officially closed to all Alaskans. Unfortunately, the word arrived hours after the skin boat had already reached the Chukotka sea. The nineteen Diomeders became captives of the Soviets for a total of three months. The families left behind on Diomede worried about the welfare of their loved ones and what would become of them, until their return with the Bureau of Indian Affairs ship, the North Star, in October 1947.

Before the border closed, Alaskans and Chukchians shared both land and sea. There was plenty of game for all, even when other regions did not fare as well. In fact, the southern tip of Big Diomede was considered an oasis for hunters from the mainlands of Alaska and Chukotka and for those from the Diomedes and King Island. Seals, walruses, and whales migrated in abundance, passing the southern tip of Big Diomede.

For many years, one could only gaze at this site and reminisce about those crystal-clear days when women from Little Diomede used to paddle to Big Diomede in skin boats to harvest leaves, roots, and berries not found on their own island. And for centuries, families from both Alaska and Chukotka voyaged between the Bering and Chukchi Seas to visit relatives and friends, to trade goods or needed supplies, and to hunt animals.

The Ice Curtain, as it was called by many, was an appropriate name for the border. The curtain erased our ability to know our relatives and cut in half the lands and seas that were once bountiful for all. It left the Alaskan and Siberian Natives with their hands outstretched but not quite touching. It caught the hunter with his right foot on one piece of ice in his own country and his left foot on another piece of ice across the border. He was forced to withdraw his step and was made to accept a bureaucratic decision from afar.

Discrimination, a Reality in Alaska

Karla Rogers   Yup'ik   Kotzebue

Most people assume that Alaska has always enjoyed racial harmony, but that isn't true. In fact, Alaska Natives were segregated at one time in Alaska just as African Americans endured segregation in the Lower 48. Discrimination experienced by Alaska Natives and African Americans was remarkably similar, including the way at least one Native stood up to Alaska's segregation laws.

In 1944, seventeen-year-old Iñupiaq Alberta Schenck went to Nome's Dream Theater on a date with an Army sergeant. As an article in *We Alaskans*, the *Anchorage Daily News* magazine, tells the story, the couple chose to sit on the side of the aisle reserved for whites. Alaska Natives were supposed to sit on the other side. The theater manager stormed down the aisle, ordered Schenck to move, and after she refused, the manager left the theater and returned with the Nome chief of police. After Schenck again refused to move, the policeman dragged her out of the theater.

Alberta Schenck refused to be treated differently than whites and was hauled off to jail. Then in 1945, the territorial legislature finally outlawed racial discrimination in Alaska but not before decades of unequal treatment under the laws.

Schenck knew what she was doing, according to *Anchorage Daily News* writer Doug O'Harra, for she had worked at Nome's Dream Theater as an usher whose duties included making sure Natives didn't sit in the "white" seats. Schenck had been fired after she confronted the manager about this policy. Afterward, Schenck had complained to the commander of the Territorial Guard, had written the *Nome Nugget* a letter about the policy, and then had gotten thrown in jail for sitting in the "white" section. Ultimately, though, after her defiance of segregation in 1944, many Natives started sitting in the Dream Theater's white section. Schenck had won a victory for equality.

Eleven years after this incident in Nome, Rosa Parks decided to sit in the front of the bus in Montgomery, Alabama. It was 1955. The law required blacks to sit in the back of the bus. When a white lady came on the bus, Parks was ordered to move but she refused. A policeman arrested Parks and took her to jail because she was breaking state segregation laws. When local blacks of Montgomery heard that Parks was taken to jail, they boycotted the bus system. They, too, believed that they should be treated the same as whites, and eventually Montgomery's bus system was integrated.

Both these incidents portray women in acts of courage and defiance. Alberta Schenck sat in the "white" section just like Rosa Parks. They both were ordered to move, then taken to jail. The Natives of Nome had followed Schenck's lead just as the blacks of Montgomery had boycotted the bus system.

Historically, laws and local "customs" segregated Natives from whites throughout Alaska. According to Terrence Cole, an associate professor of history at the University of Alaska Fairbanks, stores and restaurants in Anchorage had signs that said "No Natives Allowed," and a general store in Sitka had two entrances, one for Natives and one for whites. Whenever mining camps or settlements sprang up, according to Cole, Natives were generally cut off from participating in the economic boom and lived in shantytowns on the outskirts. Native children in Alaska attended separate schools, where they were often punished, including beatings, for speaking their own language or behaving in an "uncivilized" fashion.

Many of these incidents show that Natives were treated unequally, just as African Americans were unfairly treated in the Lower 48. Over the past 250 years, white Alaskans have often discriminated against nonwhite Alaskans, particularly Natives, with practices that included blatant racism such as social segregation. Today Alaska Natives are not subject to open discrimination, although far more subtle hints of racism still persist: for instance, in urban areas, landlords avoiding renting to Natives and not getting caught or clerks in stores treating Natives as if they are either suspicious or invisible.

Today many people still have to live with discrimination, but society has at least eliminated most legalized racism.

Adult Child of Alcoholic
Offers Hope for Herself, Others

Rebecca Gallen   *Athabascan   Northway*

Northway •

When I first heard the term, "adult child of an alcoholic," I recall feeling that I had survived growing up in an alcoholic home and didn't need to know any more about the subject. After all, I reasoned, that was the past, not the present, and certainly not the future.

However, over time, I learned more as I listened ever more closely to a friend and tried to understand why her own childhood was afflicting her so much.

Initially, I had thought her experience did not relate to anything I had known. In fact, neither of her parents drank, so I could not understand why alcohol had affected her so much. Instead, she was raised by a parent who had grown up in an alcoholic home. Also, my friend was an only child, and I was the oldest in a family of eight children. I thought that by seeking counseling my good friend was overreacting to her emotional problems.

Gradually, however, my friend helped me realize that an adult child of an alcoholic risks passing on destructive personality characteristics from one generation to the next. Finally, I began to understand the potential impact on my own children if I did not make some changes.

Even though I am not an alcoholic myself, the alcoholic home I grew up in was affecting how I was raising my children. That realization launched me into reading, taking classes, and exploring further these issues along with my friend. I wanted to learn as much as possible so I would not pass negative traits on to my own children. I wanted to break the cycle.

Many of us who grew up in alcoholic homes don't know what a "normal" family is. We may never know, but we can seek out ways to improve ourselves if family and parenting hold great personal importance. Consequently, I am always looking for articles and books on parenting and alcohol's effects in families. Two books that helped me in the beginning were *Potato Chips for Breakfast* by Cynthia G. Scales and *Keeping Secrets* by Suzanne Somers. I could identify with the real situations described in these books. In *Keeping Secrets*, the author said she did not have self-esteem, nor could she deal with the hurt and anger that came from growing up in an alcoholic home. Later, *Lifeskills for Adult Children* by Janet G. Woititz Ed.D., and Allan Garner M.A., gave me ideas about how to work through some of my confusion. One of the chapters in this book deals with expressing feelings and accepting compliments—skills that were missing in my early life.

Growing up, I thought drinking at every celebration was "normal." Meanwhile, television programs such as *Leave It To Beaver* or *Ozzie and Harriet* portrayed families that were happy all the time.

Today, I still have to work at changing some of the destructive habits I learned growing up. For example, as the oldest child, I became an "adult" very fast. I did not feel comfortable playing as a child, a feeling that stayed with me when I became a parent. I found that while I could watch and direct children on how to play, I could not get down on their level and play with them. When my boys would start wrestling, for example, I tended to stop them instead of just letting them be boys. In recent years, I have forced myself to play games with my children or other children. Today, when my youngest son wants to play a game of cards, I find myself making the time to do it, or I suggest it on my own. This may sound simple, but I consider it a great personal victory.

Adult children of alcoholics also feel they must control the lives of those around them. After a childhood of chaos and not knowing what was going to happen next, I wanted more than anything for my life to be organized. I also wanted things to happen as I thought they should. I wanted those around me to do what I expected them to do. As a mother, I unconsciously tried to control my children.

I realize now how this stifled their creativity and ability to have their own thoughts. I began to understand this as I butted heads with my fourteen-year-old, realizing we could not have a conversation without arguing. After I understood this, I tried to keep my mouth shut and listen. Now we get along better, but I still work with it.

Somewhere in my childhood mess, the important adults in my life criticized me instead of offering encouragement. As a result, I carried around low self-esteem all these years. Knowledge being power, I have since realized that I need to encourage young people and watch what I say to them, and I must read.

Recovery and discovery are an ongoing process to change what we learned as children. In the long run, I can only hope it will benefit my children for their future and for the future of their children, too.

It is possible to change.

Life Ain't Easy on Anchorage Streets for Iñupiaq from Kotzebue

Geri Reich   Iñupiaq   Kotzebue

For months he lived from day to day on the streets of downtown Anchorage, always seeking the next handful of pennies and dimes he panhandled for another much-needed drink.

His hair hung in greasy strands underneath a wide-brimmed black hat, its contours allowing his mind to help block out his dismal world.

"Ken" staggered unsteadily. A hangover from a night of drinking Papov Vodka made his legs tremble as he roamed the streets in search of fellow street friends.

Ken knew that if he begged for a few pennies here and there long enough, he eventually could buy a bottle to last him through the night. And if panhandling didn't do it, Ken had other ways to get money.

"During the summer we would snag for king salmon at the Ship Creek River, then sell it to one of the restaurants in town," he said. "That would always bring in enough cash for a cheap room at a local motel and a half-gallon of hard liquor."

Some of Ken's hometown buddies from Kotzebue also made a living on the streets. They would come along with him to make a few bucks, after Ken spread word of his plan for the day. If they were lucky to catch more than a few salmon, that would translate into a whole week of partying at a warm, cheap motel.

Kotzebue

Ken found the familiar path down the hill near Third Avenue in Anchorage that leads to a place called Tent City, a small "settlement" where most of his friends had pitched tents for Alaska's warm summer months.

"Living in those tents allowed us to stay out of the shelters," said Ken, who hates crowds. "Hundreds of homeless men and women sleep at the shelters every night, where in-house robberies of personal belongings occur frequently," he said.

A small cluster of people happily cried out to Ken as he made his way onto their turf. Other tents spread out across the grassy knoll. A Coleman stove (plastered with half-dried beans), torn blankets, dirty dishes, and empty liquor bottles lined the outside of one tent.

Five of Ken's friends agreed to go fishing with him, and they headed across the bridge to the other side of Ship Creek. As they passed Anchorage's tall glass buildings, they automatically turned to step inside the entryways to search for "snipes," which are long cigarette stubs left behind in ashtrays. None of them could afford to spend money on a pack of cigarettes, especially not when the money can be spent on something much more important.

While living on the streets of Anchorage, spending money on food is out of the question. Bean's Cafe and the Soup Kitchen, nonprofit businesses that help the homeless and the destitute in downtown Anchorage, provide at least one free meal a day. Bean's Cafe is also used as a gathering place for people to play cards as they wait for the liquor stores to open.

"The liquor stores open at 10:00 A.M. Monday through Saturday and at 12:00 noon on Sunday," said Ken, the schedule burned into his brain. "All the bars open at 10:00 A.M."

As the group made its way down to the creek, Ken, at thirty-seven, thought of when he had first attempted to befriend this group of mostly men.

At first, the group, some fifteen to twenty males, had rejected Ken. After all, he had worked a good job in the North Slope oil fields at Prudhoe Bay. Ken was not entirely like his companions. In fact, he had a clean police record. It took two months before the other guys would trust him.

"Everybody told me to go home," said Ken, whose hometown is Kotzebue, located about thirty miles inside the Arctic Circle in Northwest Alaska.

Ken had graduated at the top of his class of eighteen students from a vocational school's commercial cooking program in 1987, and had landed a job within one week, working the Prudhoe Bay oil fields that supply the trans-Alaska pipeline with its daily supply of North Slope crude.

"They fired me eight times from Prudhoe Bay," said Ken, because he could not control his drinking.

After waiting six months on probation, Ken was assigned a job in Anchorage—a job that lasted four months. It was the last job Ken would hold before his final downward spiral.

The small group of men that Ken hung around with in Anchorage soon discovered his usefulness. With no crime record, Ken could buy alcohol at any liquor store in town. Almost all of the others had been "86'd," or barred from entering liquor establishments. So Ken purchased the liquor, a valuable contribution to his group of pals.

"I knew what to buy," said Ken. "Anything that was on sale."

In addition to Ken's naturally open demeanor in talking and getting together with people, the guys made Ken their spokesperson.

"Some of the guys in our group carved ivory," he said. "They made seals, walruses, whales, kayaks, and earrings. I'd approach tourists and sell the pieces for at least twenty dollars each. They carved enough to buy a couple of half-gallons a day."

Although times were good during the summer with plenty of tourists to sell their carvings to and with schools of fish to snag at the local creek, Alaska's long dark winter arrived with harshness.

The tourists were gone. The creek was frozen solid. It was too cold to live in tents.

"During the winter, we'd go from bar to bar to stay warm, and take our bottle to the back of the bar and drink," said Ken.

Every day, the group performed what they call "hijacks" to get money. Ken, the smooth talker, would distract the downtown store clerks while one of the other guys would steal Native arts and crafts, all the time rationalizing their actions.

"We'd steal only when time was running out, when it was getting late in the evening," said Ken.

A sleep-off center in Anchorage opened its doors at 12:00 midnight every night to provide homeless drunks a safe place to sleep.

"Blood alcohol content tests were administered by personnel before anybody got to go to sleep," Ken said. If anyone was tested at having a count of over .375, she or he was transported to the Alaska Native Medical Center for observation.

According to state law, .100 is considered too drunk to drive a motor vehicle safely. Ken said he tested as high as .400, .475, and .520.

He twice admitted himself to Clitheroe, an Anchorage detoxification center, but ultimately he ended up back on the streets.

"All I did was go back downtown, find some friends, and start drinking again," he said.

During the winter, Ken got hit by a car while crossing Fourth Avenue. He cracked his collarbone, cracked a knee, and lay unconscious in the hospital for two days. The doctor told him he was lucky to be alive because most hit-and-run victims die.

"My whole life had centered on getting the next drink," said Ken, who after eighteen months on the streets eventually returned to Kotzebue.

Ken soon got involved in local activities that used to play a huge part in his life. He found that he missed the art of traditional dancing to the chants of Elders and the beat of the Eskimo drum. He joined a local group of Kotzebue Eskimo dancers, with plans to attend the Inuit Circumpolar Conference to be held in Canada that summer.

The ICC gathering allows Native groups from all over the top of the world to come together every four years to present views on subjects concerning their lives and to celebrate their heritage. Kotzebue hosted the conference in July 1988.

Competitions for Eskimo dancing are held during the meetings to break from the seriousness of the conference and to provide the spiritual and cultural dimension of these strikingly similar indigenous peoples. Ken had won one of the competitions before for his telling of Eskimo stories through his dancing.

He went to the Inuit Circumpolar Conference in Canada in the summer of 1992 with hopes to repeat his 1988 performance by coming home with another award.

Defending Iñupiaq Traditions on Many Fronts

Charlene Agnatchiaq Ferguson   *Iñupiaq*   *Kotzebue*

When I was growing up, our family would travel by boat to my grandmother's camp to pick berries, hunt, and fish. My father, uncle, brother, and male cousins would fish and hunt while my grandmother, mother, aunt, female cousins, and I would have to gather berries, pluck ducks, filet fish, and cut caribou and moose for the winter. I did this not because I wanted to but because I knew if I didn't, I wouldn't have any Iñupiaq food that I craved. My parents passed their traditions on to me, and I want to pass those traditions on to the next generation. However, this is not the only role a contemporary Native must play. Natives today defend their land politically by continuing subsistence activities on it, by passing knowledge and traditions on, and by communicating the importance of Native subsistence to non-Natives.

These modern concerns of Natives became especially pressing in the 1960s after Alaska became the forty-ninth state on January 3, 1959. The Statehood Act recognized the rights of the Natives to lands that were used for subsistence hunting and fishing but didn't provide assurance that we Natives would be able to continue to use and occupy the land. A pioneer in fighting for the land politically in the 1960s and '70s, the editor of the *Tundra Times*, Howard Rock, understood the impact of the State now being able to choose one hundred million acres of land in Alaska. He said this: "I don't think any people would ever give up any of their land. It's their life . . . their base of operation . . . their spirit and traditions and customs. That's where the land comes in." This statement sums up the continuing need to defend our land.

Though I am of another generation than Howard Rock, young people like me have been learning how to continue the battle. For instance, when I was thirteen years old, my father brought me to

Kotzebue

Anchorage to witness the annual Alaska Federation of Natives (AFN) conference. I was amazed at all the Alaska Natives gathered in one place to defend Alaska Native rights or consider whether we should have sovereignty rights. This meeting annually gives Natives a chance to voice their concerns and communicate with others. This opportunity gave me a chance to see Native leaders in action and learn from them. Later, at the age of seventeen, I went to AFN to represent Kotzebue High School, and once there, I was chosen by a group to speak to five hundred of my peers, adults and Elders about keeping our traditions.

We Natives today, however, don't just talk about traditions. We live them. For instance, from the age of twelve to eighteen years, I went to work for the NANA region's Native corporation, in a variety of jobs. I worked at Church Rock to help clip off antlers and tag the baby caribou (fawns). I was an Eskimo dancer at the NANA museum. I was a camp counselor at the Sivunigvik spirit camp where we taught Iliqusiat values to the younger generations of Iñupiat. These experiences kept me in touch with Elders who taught me my Native heritage.

I plan to continue to help with Native Alaskan issues, and the only way I see myself doing that is by going to college. Besides using this education to defend Native issues, I also want an education to be able to communicate with and persuade non-Natives that we need to protect our land, language, customs, and traditions.

On a more personal level, I want to have children someday and want them to have all the benefits I enjoyed when I was young. I want them to learn how to pick berries, pluck ducks, filet fish, and cut caribou and moose (so I don't have to!). I want my children to understand all aspects of the Iñupiaq language and knowledge. I want them to appreciate the traditional roles of Iñupiaq people but also the necessity of being politically involved, in a way that is different from generations before them.

To me a Native Iñupiaq today is someone who is preserving our land, language, and knowledge, and who is working any way he or she can to pass these traditions on to our children.

New Paths, Old Ways
Contrast for Iñupiaq Student

Verné Seum   Iñupiaq   Kiana

·Kiana

My mother and grandfather are people whom I love very much. Both are full-blooded Iñupiaq Eskimos. Nevertheless, they exhibit definite contrasts, reflecting two different eras.

My grandfather, a man of sixty-two years, is characterized by white hair and a stoic face. He has stern, piercing eyes that seem to read the thoughts and the souls of those with whom he speaks. He conserves his smiles for moments of true satisfaction, in which he celebrates quietly. His five-foot, ten-inch, 210-pound frame commands the utmost respect from those around him. He believes questions are unnecessary and that learning through observing accomplishes understanding. At this point in his life, my grandfather kicks back and enjoys his retirement.

My mother, at forty-one, has deep black hair that complements her compassionate face. Her gentle, loving smile is mirrored by the luster of her glistening black eyes. She is an outgoing, witty woman who is proud of her heritage. She has a petite build of five feet, two inches, and weighs 104 pounds. Unlike my grandfather, my mother's views are contemporary. She believes that in order to avoid confusion, verbal communication is necessary. Far from retirement, my mother loves working.

My grandfather, after raising children for forty-one years, now leaves that chore behind him. He still makes his opinions on raising children known: His conservative ideas on education lead him to believe that children should learn at home with their families. In this case, chores take first priority over extracurricular activities.

Far different, my mother, in raising five children, encourages obtaining formal education to supplement life's experiences. Her goal is that we continue our education after high school. To her, homework always comes first.

The conflicting influences these two individuals bestow upon my life often cause problems. My mother, liberated and independent, has one son in his freshman year of college, a daughter in her last year of high school and enrolled in college courses, and a daughter in seventh grade moving ahead scholastically and determined to go to college. My mother always pushes us to do our best in school.

In complete contrast to my mother's modern views, my grandfather believes that women have their duties and should be submissive. Influenced by my grandfather, my brother has learned some of the traditional ways of hunting and fishing. In my grandfather's household, my sister and I maintain the house and cook for our uncles. We also have learned that we have to budget our time effectively, because he feels we spend too much time at school and at school activities.

Here are two people that I love dearly, but what a contrast!

My grandfather lives in a time past, a time when tradition was the only way to survive, when education could only be taught through informal means, and a time when women and men had definite roles that insured the survival of the people. To him, this life is secure. He fails to understand why our generation can't live the life he has led.

My mother, however, remembers the past, lives for today, and prepares for tomorrow. She doesn't ignore tradition but insists that we be able to adjust to new conditions. To her, the world is modern, where acceleration and advancement are the means of survival. She believes the way to advance is to increase one's education in the formal classroom. She lives the life of an independent woman.

To her, to be educated is to be secure.

Chores Should Be Equally Divided at Home

Anthony Lincoln   Iñupiaq   Kotzebue

•Kotzebue

Children who grow up doing chores equally with their brothers or sisters will most likely maintain those values throughout life. I don't think it's fair for either women or men to do the majority of the chores in the household or at the workplace. It takes two to marry and have kids, so it should take two to do everything to earn a decent living, keep a clean household, and raise children responsibly.

Equality is, simply, the quality or state of being equal. Household chores, however, are not always divided up equally, although things have changed in many homes in America since author Judy Syfers wrote her essay in 1971, titled "I Want a Wife." Syfers described how she was treated like a slave to her husband. She wrote how she would "have to do all the basic chores" and be there for him whenever he needed her.

Today most families in Kotzebue find men going to work and coming home to dinner on the table. Most women work, also, and so most mothers must rush home to start cooking each night. In addition, the women in Kotzebue still do most household chores, from cooking and cleaning to caring for the children.

Historically, most women stayed home to take care of the children, while the men worked tiring, labor-intensive jobs. Historically, women didn't normally work construction or labor-intensive work, but in recent years, women have been moving into nontraditional jobs outside the home. Social historian Barbara Dafoe Whitehead writes in her book, Family Affairs, that "today's at-home mother may be tomorrow's working mom." With women working outside the home, this is changing society in Kotzebue as well as across America.

"Due to changes in career opportunities and the relaxation of traditional societal roles, children today are not being raised as their parents were," writes author Philip Elmer-Dewitt in The Great Experiment.

It puts a lot of stress on the man or woman who is responsible for doing all the household chores, plus a job outside the home. Author Penelope Leach writes in her book, Your Baby and Child, "Home and its surrounding community used to be everybody's operating base, with work and play and family pretty much intermixed," but times have changed, and men and women need to adapt.

Perhaps couples would get along better if they divided the household chores fairly. If children grow up watching both parents doing household chores equally, they'll learn that doing chores and jobs is not for punishment, but is something people have to do to maintain a normal, successful life.

Single parents especially face increased challenges raising their children, making sure chores are done and food is on the table every night, and working their job outside the home. "Today's parents are raising children in ways that little resemble their own youth," says author Elmer-Dewitt, "with day care centers and many more single-parent homes."

I've experienced a significant change myself for the past five years, living with just my mother, my two brothers, and sister. We children have learned to be "a big help" for my mother. She comes home from work and all the basic chores are done, such as vacuuming, sweeping, fixing the beds, doing dishes, and putting everything in order like shoes, books, hats, jackets, and so forth. All Mom has to do is cook.

Children living in a single-parent home or any other kind of family should help out in every way they can. Cooperation makes life that much easier, and children learn valuable skills in self-sufficiency to prepare them to become adults and parents themselves. Also, this is in keeping with the Iñupiaq value of cooperation.

• Kotzebue

Iñupiaq Woman Balances Work, Family Responsibilities

Geri Reich   Iñupiaq   Kotzebue

Sometimes as I fly out of Kotzebue to go back to work at the Red Dog Mine, I remember the first time I took this route a few years ago in July 1988, my first day on the job.

Although Red Dog's location ninety miles above the Arctic Circle brings frigid temperatures most of the year, on this brilliant summer's day, the perpetual sun's heat stifled the crowded cabin in Baker Aviation's Cessna 402 as we left Kotzebue's airport runway.

Small fishing boats bobbed in the waves below as we flew north over Kotzebue Sound. Normally, I would have been on one of those boats, commercial fishing.

Instead, I was leaving Kotzebue, the small, dusty, remote town in Northwest Alaska where I was born, where I grew up. I had agreed

Iñupiaq Geri Reich at work at Red Dog Mine, a huge lead and zinc deposit in northwestern Alaska. Circa 1993. Photo courtesy Geri Reich.

to live and work—at least for the next six months—in an even more remote place. Ambivalence crowded my mind. "What was I doing? Is all this worth my time?"

I was again leaving my two children, then eight-year-old A. J. and twelve-year-old Jennifer, for a long time. I had just completed five months of electrical training at the Alaska Vocational Technical Center in Seward, hundreds of miles from Kotzebue. I ached to be a normal mother and just stay home, baking cookies for my kids.

On that first day on the job in 1988, we landed at Red Dog on a short, rocky runway among huge, rust-colored mountains that mark the area. The expediter who met the plane herded all six of us new faces onto a bus that brought us to tents shaped like Quonset huts, where we were to live. Green Construction, one of many companies contracting with Cominco that summer, was laying the groundwork for the permanent living accommodations and the administrative services complexes.

I had been hired on as a laborer. Only later, after the buildings were erected, would I switch over to my present job as an electrician.

Some twenty years ago, as a young tomboy of ten years of age driving a pedal-starting black moped around Kotzebue's unpaved streets, I had no idea that a discovery to the north of us would so significantly carve my future and the future of my people.

That summer in 1968, Bob Baker, a bush pilot from Kotzebue, was returning home from one of his many flying trips. Looking out from his plane across the Arctic's vast wilderness, Baker noticed reddish stains in a creek amid the Delong Mountains just north of the village of Noatak in the western Brooks Range. The young pilot mentioned his unusual sighting to the U.S. Geological Survey after he arrived back in Kotzebue. This discovery would turn out to be a major find that would change this part of arctic Alaska forever.

By 1975, Cominco Alaska, a Canadian-based mining company, had selected this area north of Noatak as a potentially mineral-rich deposit. Geologists flew in to stake claims, although no one still could have guessed what a tremendous discovery this would be. Baker's faithful traveling companion on that flying trip had been O'Malley, a red Irish setter. Thus, the "Red Dog" Mine.

By the early part of 1982, Cominco had struck a massive deposit of zinc and lead. Later that same year, Cominco signed a joint-venture contract with NANA, my Native regional corporation, to develop the mine. The agreement stipulates that NANA Regional Corporation lease the land to Cominco, which in turn would agree to handle all phases of the mine's startup, operation, and sale of the mine's products.

How did NANA, and thus the Native people of this part of Alaska, gain title to the land on which the Red Dog Mine lies?

In 1971, the U.S. Congress passed the Alaska Native Claims Settlement Act, which settled the aboriginal land claims of Alaska Natives, who had hunted, fished, and gathered off Alaska's harsh, rugged landscape for thousands of years.

NANA is one of the thirteen regional corporations set up by ANCSA. The "NANA region" includes eleven Iñupiaq Eskimo villages in this mountain- and tundra-filled corner of Northwest Alaska that lies almost entirely above the Arctic Circle.

In compensation for traditional lands that Alaska Natives lost in their settlement with the federal government, ANCSA set up thirteen regional corporations and more than two hundred village corporations with the $962.5 million cash settlement, which the fledgling companies used to capitalize themselves.

In the decades since Congress passed ANCSA, NANA Regional Corporation's stated for-profit goals have been to utilize its property holdings and businesses strictly for shareholder benefit.

Our region continues to be westernized despite its 90 percent Native population. Consequently, regional leaders believe that training and employment, to take advantage of opportunities such as the Red Dog Mine, are crucial to the integration of the Iñupiaq life-style with the Western way.

Nevertheless, when my people were deciding to go ahead with the Red Dog Mine, local people at meetings held all over the NANA region questioned how opening the mine would affect our Iñupiaq culture. Echoes of fear resounded throughout the region on how the overall operation of the mine would affect local subsistence resources.

For example, the mine is located directly in the path of a large caribou herd that passes through the area to reach one of its favorite grazing grounds. The Red Dog Creek, which runs below the huge ore body that Cominco's drilling crews blast with dynamite every day, eventually flows into the Wulik River.

The Wulik, in turn, empties into the Chukchi Sea near the tiny village of Kivalina, one of the villages in the NANA region. Kivalina residents depend on the fish caught from this river.

In recent years, contamination from high levels of metal, as reported in the Alaska press, was jeopardizing the pristine Wulik River. Kivalina residents were especially concerned about the safety of their subsistence fish supply. NANA and Cominco officials subsequently met with Kivalina's apprehensive residents. Apparently, the officials allayed the fears of local people, who were told that the mine would be making changes to the flow of Red Dog Creek.

Cominco has since constructed an additional dam in an attempt to thwart dangerous levels of heavy metals from entering the Wulik. Time will be the greatest test for whether these efforts pay off.

Local people hope that the monitoring of the caribou's annual crossings and proper treatment of Red Dog Creek's water by Cominco will protect and preserve our subsistence resources. Officials continue to take samples of fish from the Wulik River. Kivalina's residents and their drinking water are also tested regularly for any sign of lead contamination.

"Like Prudhoe Bay, I wonder about the caribou," said one local Native who works for Cominco at Red Dog. "Can't help but be concerned about the caribou crossing the roadway."

Those caribou belong to the large arctic herd, which feeds off the land just as we, the Iñupiaq Eskimos, do.

According to Ron McLean, human resources manager at the Red Dog Mine, during the first two years after Cominco started hauling its product to the seaport on the newly constructed fifty-two-mile, state-funded road, no animals were hit by ore-hauling trucks.

In addition to promising to mine responsibly in an environmentally sensitive area, Cominco also has agreed to train and hire NANA shareholders for jobs at the mine.

According to Cominco, employment of NANA shareholders at Red Dog has remained between 58 percent and 60 percent since the mine operation began. Both NANA and Cominco officials predict that the Red Dog Mine will employ 100 percent Native Eskimos by its twelfth year of operation.

Training programs for electricians, mechanics, millwrights, food-service workers, and clerk typists have been offered at post-secondary technical centers in both Kotzebue and Seward. Training sessions last from six to thirteen months. Successful graduates typically finish their programs with on-the-job training at the Red Dog Mine as Cominco employees.

I am one of those former students. In January 1988, after completing introductory classes at the Alaska Technical Center in Kotzebue, I flew to Seward for basic training in electricity. Being the only female among ten other male trainees brought fear, remorse, then determination, as I settled into Seward's small-city life.

Nevertheless, being away from my children hurt. Within two weeks, I was writing poetry to ease the pain:

Sadness envelopes me today
Like the dark, wet blanket of fog
That falls over Seward
Every child I see
Reminds me of you
I long for the sunshine of home
Where it allows me always to watch over you
Soon, when the darkness lifts
We'll be together again
As we should be
I miss you
My babies.

These feelings still haunt me to this day as I travel back and forth to Red Dog from Kotzebue for my job.

The mine's work schedule goes on a four-week-on, two-week-off rotation. This was set up by Cominco to provide employees with on-the-job training without interruption, although the company has since implemented different work schedules that allow workers to go home more often. Many employees, including myself, welcome the new two-week-on, one-week-off schedule because we have children. I prefer seeing my children more often, though it may be for half as much time as before. I find that I am missing many important steps in their young lives.

For example, I was not home for the ceremony when Jennifer graduated from the eighth grade. My son is now a young hunter. When did he learn to do that? He once asked trustingly, "Mom, when are you going to quit working at Red Dog?" They have celebrated their birthdays without me. Feelings of inadequacy as a parent invade my whole body because I'm not doing what society expects of me.

Working at the Red Dog Mine for four weeks at a stretch leaves

Red Dog Mine. 1993. The mine, north of Kotzebue, began operating in 1989 and today boasts the largest zinc deposit in the Western world. Photo by Jim Magdanz.

me with full days, but empty nights. That's why I have enrolled in writing classes at Chukchi College, a branch in Kotzebue of the statewide University of Alaska system. I have always wanted to be a writer. That's what I fill many of my nights with now.

Darkness descends upon us here in the Arctic for many months out of the year, although the brief summer months shower us with almost continuous daylight.

Cominco offers many activities to alleviate the restlessness and boredom at the mine. A large gymnasium, for example, offers nights of basketball, volleyball, and badminton. A weight room, men's and women's sauna rooms, and a Jacuzzi for six to eight people are all within walking distance. Cable television enters every private room, providing eleven channels, including Home Box Office. In addition, Kotzebue's local radio station offers regional news and events from the NANA region as well as state and national news.

Cominco also sponsors contests for its employees. For example, the Red Dog Ice Classic resembles the Nenana Ice Classic, a contest in Interior Alaska that awards huge sums each year — $140,000 in 1991 — for the most accurate prediction for the ice going out at a certain point on the Nenana River. The Red Dog Ice Classic uses the ice breakup each spring of a nearby pond. The contest has spawned local "experts" in ice formation. One year the prize was a round trip for two to Hawaii. The next year, the lucky winner traveled to Mexico.

Another company-sponsored contest once offered a "reward" of $500 to four employees who best named our accommodations complex, or the place we call home away from home. We all now live in the "Dog House."

Such activities help workers make it through long days of working and being away from their families amid our limited existence at the mine.

For example, many outside activities are restricted because of the blasting of dynamite that occurs a scant half-mile from where we work and live, and Red Dog is an "open-pit" mine because of its deposits' proximity to the surface of the earth.

Despite such restrictions, roadways and trails are available for walks and sightseeing. During deep winter, though, most residents usually remain inside Red Dog's buildings, sometimes never setting foot outside for weeks at a time. During one hitch one winter, for instance, I did not dare go outside for five weeks, as the Arctic's typically frigid temperatures remained far, far below zero.

Because of its location in the extreme Far North, Red Dog was built with the utmost consideration for the Arctic's legendary cold. Long utilidors connect every main building, so the walk or "daily commute" from my room in the Dog House to my job station takes no more than a few minutes. I never have to go outside, which is okay with me in winter.

In contrast to the pitch black of winter's nights and days, summers offer festive outdoor picnics when the kitchen staff prepares hot dogs, hamburgers, and fried chicken. Almost everyone looks forward to these different meals, since usually we have Sunday-night prime rib, Wednesday-night New York steak, and the never-ending Friday-night seafood platter.

Cominco also provides to its Native employees a small dining room for the enjoyment of Iñupiaq food. Upon returning to Red Dog from their villages, many workers bring in delicacies of Eskimo food such as frozen fish, seal oil, caribou jerky, and whale and seal meat. The room provides a place for local Eskimos to get together to share family and regional news. The gathering elicits closeness and sharing of traits for which the Iñupiat are known.

The Red Dog Mine, at the present time, is considered to be the largest zinc and lead mine in the free world. An estimated 2.1 million tons of reserves are processed each year. After the ore is reduced to a concentrate, eighty-two-ton trucks haul the concentrate to a newly built seaport fifty-two miles away. Since shipping season is only ninety to one hundred days per year, a building the size of six football fields (which flies the Alaska flag from its roof) holds the product during the winter.

When spring comes and the frozen Chukchi Sea melts, ships sail into the seaport to carry the concentrate away to faraway places such as Canada, Japan, and Europe. Geologists estimate that the mine will supply Cominco with zinc and lead for the next fifty years.

That means that my grandchildren may well have the same career opportunities that I have now, although I wonder if they, too, will ache just to stay home with their kids.

Glossary

This glossary lists common "Alaskanisms" such as the word "sno-go" for a snowmachine as well as Iñupiaq and Yup'ik words commonly used in rural areas. Other relevant place names and terms are included.

Note: Iñupiaq is spoken by Iñupiaq Eskimos of northern and northwestern Alaska. Central Alaskan Yup'ik is spoken by Yup'ik Eskimos in southwestern Alaska.

aana: Iñupiaq word for grandmother.

akutuq: Iñupiaq word for Eskimo ice cream, typically consisting of whipped fat from caribou, reindeer or moose, mixed with shredded white fish, a little seal oil, and blended berries. Yup'ik word is *akutaq*.

atikłuq: Iñupiaq word for a hooded top garment, often made with calico material.

iglu: Iñupiaq word for a sod house. Also refers to a beaver home or mouse home.

kuspuk: from the Yup'ik word, *qaspeq*, meaning a hooded top garment, often made of calico material.

mukluk: from the Yup'ik word for bearded seal, *maklaq*, to mean boots, generally made out of sealskin, caribou leg skin, or calfskin.

muktuk: from the Iñupiaq for outer flesh of bowhead or beluga whale, including the blubber, which is eaten frozen, fresh, cooked, or pickled. Proper Iñupiaq spelling is *maktak* or *maptak*.

naluaġmiu: Iñupiaq word for white man, meaning "people of bleached seal skin."

niqipiaq: Iñupiaq or Native food.

paniqtaq: Iñupiaq word for dried meat.

paniqtuq: Iñupiaq word for dried fish.

qayaq: Iñupiaq and Yup'ik word for kayak.

quaġaq: Iñupiaq word for sourdock, an edible green.

quaq: Iñupiaq word for frozen fish.

sno-go: commonly used term for a snowmobile or snowmachine.

taata: Iñupiaq word for grandfather.

taikuułallak: Iñupiaq word meaning "many thanks."

tuttulik: Iñupiaq word for a soft-bottomed mukluk (see above).

ugruk: Iñupiaq word for bearded seal and its meat.

ulu: Iñupiaq for cutting knife with curved blade. In Yup'ik, ulu means "tongue," and the knife is called *uluaq*.

umiaq: Iñupiaq word for lightweight skin boats used by coastal Eskimos; boats were covered with walrus or bearded seal hides.

About the Contributors

Shona Greist Andrews, "Iñupiaq Recipe for Cooking and Gathering Sourdock." Iñupiaq Shona Griest Andrews, Iñupiaq name Nasruluk, was born July 22, 1977, in Kotzebue. She wrote her piece while a student at Kotzebue High School attending college classes. She also spent two semesters at Chemawa High School in Oregon. She was a Resource Apprenticeship Student for two summers during high school, getting hands-on experience in natural resources management. A particularly favorite area of study was botony, an interest that led to her piece about the plant sourdock for this volume. She also has had heavy-equipment operation training. Shona especially enjoys choral singing. She is married to Yup'ik Aaron Naulaq Andrews from the village of Aleknagik. Her mother, Hannah Paniyavluk Loon, is another contributor to this anthology.

Dolly Arnold, "Sisters Incorporate Traditional Values in Modern Pursuits." Iñupiaq Dolly Arnold was born on March 15, 1965, in Noorvik, a village about forty-five miles northeast of Kotzebue. She wrote her piece while living in Kotzebue. She is a 1984 graduate of Selawik High School in Selawik, Alaska, a village in northwest Alaska to the east of Kotzebue.

Linda Akeya, "How to Skin a Polar Bear." Siberian Yup'ik Linda Akeya was born May 18, 1967, in Anchorage. She wrote this selection while working toward an education degree, so that she could teach elementary school in the village of Savoonga on St. Lawrence Island in the Bering Sea, or elsewhere in Alaska. She grew up in a family of nine children and learned the Siberian Yup'ik dialect, Eskimo dancing, and hunting games from her parents.

Rena Boolowon Booshu, "Remembering Grandfather" and "Components of a Traditional Siberian Yup'ik Marriage." Siberian Yup'ik Rena Boolowon Booshu was born September 18, 1969, in Nome. She wrote her pieces while living a subsistence life-style in Gambell, Alaska, a village on St. Lawrence Island in the Bering Sea. She was attending college part-time to pursue a degree in rural development from the University of Alaska in order to specialize in small-village-corporation management. She grew up in a family of six, gathering greens and berries with her mother and sometimes hunting and boating with her father.

Benjamin Brantley, "A First-Hand Account of the Kotzebue Water System Freeze-Up." Iñupiaq Ben Brantley, Iñupiaq name Uvigaq, was born on May 22, 1960, in Kotzebue. He was working for Kotzebue's public works department when he wrote this story. He later went on to work for the newly opened NAPA Auto Parts store in Kotzebue. He has lived in several places in Alaska, including Yakutat in southeastern Alaska and Anchorage. He is a graduate of East Anchorage High School.

John Cleveland, "Quick Meal of Muskrat Serves As Nourishment on the Trail." Iñupiaq John Cleveland was born February 4, 1965, in Selawik. He is a 1983 graduate of Selawik High School, where he played basketball and edited the school newspaper. He joined the U.S. Army after high school and later worked at Red Dog Mine in northwestern Alaska as a laborer.

Blanche Jones "B. J." Criss, "Brother's Battle with Cancer Sends Sister Home" and "When People Carrying Bibles Came." Iñupiaq Blanche Jones "B. J." Criss was born March 16, 1949, in Kotzebue. One of thirteen children, she lived much of her childhood with her great-grandparents and mother and stepfather, Dora and Claude Wilson, at Sisualik, a subsistence camp nine miles across the water from coastal Kotzebue. She graduated from Nome Beltz High School in Nome, Alaska, later working in the oil industry across the United States. She wrote these recollections while living in Kotzebue but has since moved to Point Hope, an Eskimo whaling village in northwestern Alaska. B.J. was one of two students who traveled to the home of Ethel Kennedy in McLean, Virginia, in May 1991, to accept the Robert F. Kennedy Journalism Award for Outstanding Coverage of the Problems of the Disadvantaged, on behalf of her fellow student writers who participated in 1990 in the Chukchi News and Information Service publication project, from which this anthology is created.

Lucy Daniels, "Writer Grows Up Eskimo in 'Ancient' Alaska," "Learning about White, Middle-Class America in Rural Alaska," and "Death, a Part of Life." Yup'ik Lucy Daniels, Yup'ik name Nuqarrluk, born September 26, 1946, in Bethel, Alaska, was living in Elim near Nome in northwestern Alaska when she wrote her selections in a journalism class. She grew up in a family of nine children, supplementing a diet of fish and game with store-bought food. A home-maker, Lucy is married to Jerry Daniels and has a daughter and a son.

Jimmie Evak, "Using Pallets to Warm Your Home." Iñupiaq Jimmie Evak was born on February 13, 1955, in Kotzebue. He was working in Kotzebue for the Alaska Department of Fish and Game, Subsistence Division, when he wrote this piece and subsequently moved to Anchorage to train as a carpenter. He is a 1973 graduate of Kotzebue High School and a 1987 graduate of Chukchi Community College, with an A.A. in liberal arts.

Charlene Ferguson, "Defending Iñupiaq Traditions on Many Fronts." Iñupiaq Charlene Ferguson, Iñupiaq name Agnatchiaq, was born on December 15, 1967, in Kotzebue, and grew up in an Iñupiaq family of four children whose upbringing included spending summers hunting, fishing, and gathering. During the school year she and her siblings witnessed the political environment of Juneau, where her father, Frank Ferguson, served as a state legislator. At the time this selection was written, she was working toward a bachelor's degree in business administration at Chukchi College in Kotzebue with the goal of working for a Native corporation. Her education has since taken her to the main University of Alaska campuses in Fairbanks and Anchorage.

Rebecca Gallen, "Adult Child of Alcoholic Offers Hope for Herself, Others." Athabascan Rebecca Gallen was born July 14, 1949, in Tanana, a village on the Yukon River in interior Alaska. She wrote of her experiences while working as a Johnson O'Malley counselor and while pursuing a bachelor's degree in secondary education from the home she shares with her husband, James, in Northway, forty-two miles west of the Canadian border. She plans to teach or counsel high school students. She grew up in a family of eight children and is a parent to four boys.

James Gooden, "Life's Journey around the Country and Back to Kiana" and "Iñupiaq Relates Hard Times in Elementary School in the 1950s." Iñupiaq James Gooden, birth name Ronald Andrews Tobuk, was born on July 14, 1946, in Fairbanks. He was working as a teacher's aide in his home village of Kiana in northwestern Alaska when he wrote these personal stories. Subsequently he headed for the North Slope oil fields to work security for a subsidiary of NANA, his Native regional corporation. He is a 1967 graduate of Chemawa Indian School in Oregon, and a 1969 graduate of Haskell Institute (now Haskell Indian Nations University) in Kansas, as well as a Vietnam-era veteran (U.S. Navy, Navy corpsman, 1969–71). He completed village public safety officer training at the police academy in Sitka, Alaska, in 1973 and later served in the Alaska National Guard. Besides having worked as a police officer, security officer, Bureau of Land Management emergency firefighter, and teacher aide in special education, Indian education, and migrant education, he has served on the northwest arctic region's Maniilaq Board of Directors, as well as on the Kiana Traditional Council Board. Other positions he has held in Kiana include mayor and magistrate. He is a father of four.

Sheila Gregg, "Teller Misled Alaskans on Project Chariot." Iñupiaq Sheila Gregg, born on February 4, 1973, wrote this story while working as a teacher's aide and secretary in Deering, a coastal village south of Kotzebue on the Kotzebue Sound. She also has worked as a community health practitioner. A mother of two children, she particularly remembers the lessons of her Elders, who taught her how to make calfskin mukluks and beaver hats, as well as how to cut up seal and fish.

Calvin "Sonny" Harris, "Writer Includes Self in Definition of Computer Nerd." Iñupiaq Calvin "Sonny" Harris, Inupiaq name Ikkitchiiq, was born on June 6, 1954, at a camp near Kotzebue, Sisualik. He wrote this selection while attending college classes and raising four children with his wife, Jan. He completed his GED in 1982 and today is employed by Maniilaq Health Center, the public health hospital in Kotzebue, where he continues to enjoy computers, especially since the more prominent presence of the Internet.

Carol Harris, "How to Make Seal Oil." Iñupiaq Carol Harris was born May 5, 1958, in Kotzebue. She has worked as assistant accounts receivable manager for Maniilaq Health Center in Kotzebue as well as business manager for KOTZ radio, the AM station serving Kotzebue and the northwestern arctic region of Alaska. She grew up in a family of three children, living a traditional Iñupiaq life style. She completed her GED in 1984 and has since taken college classes.

Dollie Hawley, "Growing Up in Kivalina on Alaska's Remote Arctic Coast." Iñupiaq Dollie Hawley, Iñupiaq name Ahyahlooktook, was born March 18, 1955, in Kivalina, a coastal village to the north of Kotzebue. Dollie completed a GED in 1976 and has since taken college classes. Dollie has worked as a nurse's aide and a radio announcer at KOTZ-AM, the public station serving northwestern

Alaska. She grew up in a family of ten children and has one child of her own.

Helena Hildreth, "Making Jam from Fresh Tundra Berries Recalls Memories." Iñupiaq/Yup'ik Helena Hildreth was born on October 23, 1963, in Unalakleet, a village in the Nome region on the Norton Sound. She wrote this selection while living in Kotzebue, where she was working for the Alaska Department of Community and Regional Affairs. She currently is staying home with her three children while continuing to attend college classes. She is a 1981 graduate of Covenant High School in Unalakleet. She grew up in a family of ten children.

Tina Maria Jones, "Iñupiaq Grows Up Traveling with the Seasons." Iñupiaq Tina Jones was born November 1, 1962, in Kotzebue, where she was living when she wrote this piece. She completed a GED in 1983 and has since taken college classes. Her childhood was spent primarily on subsistence activities in northwestern Alaska.

Anthony Lincoln, "Chores Should Be Equally Divided at Home." Iñupiaq Tony Lincoln, born June 25, 1977, in Kotzebue, wrote this essay while a student at Kotzebue High School. He was also attending college classes and busy with school sports. After graduating in 1996, he planned to undergo training to become a state trooper in Alaska. In the meantime, he has been working at the Red Dog Mine in northwestern Alaska to help pay for that training.

Georgianna Lincoln, "Lack of True American Indian History in Textbooks." Athabascan Georgianna Lincoln, born February 22, 1943, in Fairbanks, wrote this essay while living in Rampart, a tiny Athabascan Indian settlement on a remote stretch of the Yukon River. Since 1976, she has been a board member of Doyon, Ltd., her Native regional corporation (and America's largest private landholder). She also is past president of Baan O Yeel Kon, her Native village corporation, is a former bank board member, and was pursuing a bachelor's degree in public administration via distance education from her village when in 1990 she successfully ran for the state House of Representatives. She became Alaska's first Native female state senator in 1992. A Democrat, Senator Lincoln has championed concerns that include adequate sanitation facilities in Native villages, rural Alaska subsistence hunting and fishing rights, full funding for education, and children and women's issues. She has also been a candidate for Alaska's lone seat in the U. S. House of Representatives.

Hannah Loon, "Remember Me," "Iñupiaq Woman Learns How to Search for Mouse Caches," and "Village English Spoken by Young and Old in Rural Alaska." Iñupiaq Hannah Loon, Iñupiaq name Paniyavluk, was born May 8, 1949, near Selawik, a village to the east of Kotzebue along the Selawik River. She wrote of her experiences while working for the Alaska Department of Fish and Game as a resource specialist. She currently is employed as Special Assistant to the Board of Directors for NANA Regional Corporation in Kotzebue. Hannah grew up in a family of four children, whose lives were busy with subsistence activities. Hannah was one of two students who traveled to the home of Ethel Kennedy in McLean, Virginia, in May 1991, to accept the Robert F. Kennedy Journalism Award for Outstanding Coverage of the Problems of the Disadvantaged, on behalf of her fellow student writers who participated in 1990 in the Chukchi News and Information Service publication project, from which this anthology is created. She is the mother of Shona Greist Andrews, another contributor to this volume.

Eva Menadelook, "Growing Up in the Shadow of the Ice Curtain." Iñupiaq Eva Menadelook was born January 26, 1957, on Little Diomede, a small island in the Bering Sea across from the former Soviet-held island of Big Diomede. She wrote her essay about growing up in her home community across from the Soviet Union just prior to the melting of the Ice Curtain that came with the break-up of the Soviet Union in the early 1990s. She comes from a family of five children with parents who taught her and her siblings how to harvest, preserve, and prepare sea mammals such as ugruk (bearded seal), walrus, and spotted and harbor seals. She received her GED in 1978 and at this writing was working as Itinerant Community Health Practitioner out of Nome, for the Norton Sound Health Corporation.

Genevieve Norris, "Subsistence Means Keeping Busy Year-Round." Iñupiaq Genny Norris was born on December 10, 1947, in Shungnak, a village east of Kotzebue on the Kobuk River. She wrote "Subsistence Means Keeping Busy Year-Round" while working as a village coordinator for the Maniilaq Alcohol Program and pursuing college classes in social work.

Spencer Rearden, "Waterfowl Hunter's Dream Pursued by Family," "Fox Snaring, a Painstaking Art," and "Families Help Define the Meaning of 'Native.'" Yup'ik Spencer Rearden, born January 4, 1979, in Kodiak, Alaska, wrote these stories while a high school sophomore at Kotzebue High School, attending college classes. He comes from a tradition of writing, his paternal grandfather being a frequently published outdoors writer. He has since returned to southwestern Alaska to finish his secondary schooling in Bethel. He has three siblings and plans to have a career in wildlife management.

Geri Reich, "Small Aircraft Flight Turns Silent after Frightening Experience," "Life Ain't Easy on Anchorage Streets for Iñupiaq from Kotzebue," and "Iñupiaq Woman Balances Work, Family Responsibilities." Iñupiaq Geri Reich, born June 6, 1958, in Kotzebue, is a mother of two who wrote her essays while working as an electrician at the remote Red Dog Mine, a massive lead-and-zinc deposit in northwestern Alaska, located about eighty air miles north of Kotzebue. Geri completed her journeyman's license while also attending academic classes, primarily in order to pursue a journalism degree. She grew up in a family of six children, spending summers at a subsistence camp across the Kotzebue Sound and living in Kotzebue in the winters to attend school.

Karla Rogers, "Discrimination, a Reality in Alaska." Yup'ik Karla Rogers, born October 16, 1978, in Kotzebue, wrote this essay while a junior at Kotzebue High School and a participant in an honors program at Chukchi College. She also plays the saxophone and was a member of her school's volleyball team. She has since graduated from Kotzebue High School and gone on to attend the University of Alaska Fairbanks. Her essay has won an Honorable Mention in the Robert. F. Kennedy Journalism Awards for Outstanding Coverage of the Problems of the Disadvantaged. She plans on studying international business, possibly in the field of foreign relations. She grew up in a family of four children.

Sandra Russell, "My Experience on the Blanket Toss." Iñupiaq Sandy Russell, a mother of four, was working as an administrative assistant at Chukchi College in Kotzebue, where she was also pursuing an associate of arts degree. She grew up with both her mother and father working jobs outside the home along with subsistence activities. As a child, she spent summers at her grandmother's cabin on the Noatak River picking berries as well as cutting and drying fish for their winter food supply.

Wilfred "Boyuck" Ryan, "A Boat's-Eye View of Fishing on the Norton Sound." Iñupiaq Wilfred "Boyuck" Ryan, born April 10, 1953, in Unalakleet, Alaska, in the Nome region, wrote this story about commercial fishing while pursuing a bachelor's degree in business administration and working as a pilot and travel manager out of Unalakleet. He grew up in a family of nine children in a traditional subsistence life-style supplemented by the cash economy.

Ruthie Sampson, "Iñupiaq Educator Provides Link between Elders and Students." Iñupiaq Ruthie Sampson was born October 18, 1954, in Selawik, Alaska, a village inland from Kotzebue. She wrote this selection while working as Bilingual Education Coordinator for the Northwest Arctic Borough School District, a job that includes publishing bilingual books for the region's students. She grew up in a family of seven children, going to school in the winter and camping and living off the land in the summer. Her parents spoke Iñupiaq to her. She attended high school in Anchorage and graduated in 1972. She has four children and is married to a dog musher.

Mildred Savok, "My Life As I Remember It." Iñupiaq Millie Savok, Iñupiaq name Aviiksaq, was born February 2, 1953, in Kotzebue. At the time she wrote of her experiences, she was working as an administrative assistant for Maniilaq Association, a nonprofit social service organization in Kotzebue. Her academic goals include pursuing a degree in social work or business management. She is a mother of five who, besides parenting, enjoys traveling to the Lower 48, drawing, and bingo. She grew up in a family of four children, whose subsistence activities included picking berries and fishing. Today, she continues to fish either through the ice or with rod and reel.

Verné Seum, "New Paths, Old Ways Contrast for Iñupiaq Student." Iñupiaq Verné Seum was born July 4, 1971, in Torrance, California. She wrote her essay while a high school senior in Kiana, as part of Kotzebue-based Chukchi College's outreach program for promising regional secondary students, who can earn college credit while still in high school. Her extracurricular activities included holding a spot on the girls' basketball team. Kiana lies above the Arctic Circle in northwestern Alaska, on the banks of the upper Kobuk River. A graduate of Kiana High School, Verné went on to attend the University of Alaska Fairbanks before transferring to Portland State University in Oregon, where at this writing she has nearly completed a bachelor's degree in business management, emphasizing information systems and quantitative analysis. During her college years, Verné also lived six months in Germany; worked several student internships in Anchorage at NANA, her Native regional corporation;

and also worked with American Indian and other Native peoples in the Lower 48 through the Northewest Portland Area Indian Health Board in Oregon. Upon graduation, Verné plans to continue to work with Native peoples "whether it be within my career or outside of my job," in either Alaska or the Pacific Northwest.

Kathleen Uhl Sherman, "Tundra Beckons throughout Life." Iñupiaq Kathleen Uhl Sherman, born on June 20, 1971, in Kotzebue, wrote this essay about the tundra while working for the Alaska Department of Fish and Game in Kotzebue. She grew up in a family of four children, who she says continue to hunt and gather traditional foods while holding down full-time jobs.

Rachel Sherman, "Bear Scare." Iñupiaq Rachel Sherman was born September 30, 1946, in Noatak, Alaska, a village north of Kotzebue on the Noatak River. She wrote this story while teaching the Iñupiaq language in the Noatak village school. She grew up in a family of twelve children and has pursued traditional subsistence activities with her husband and children in Noatak most of her life. She completed an Alaska Native Language Certificate in May 1996.

John Stalker, "Geese Hunting Provides Valuable Lesson." Iñupiaq John Stalker, born January 30, 1977, in Kotzebue, wrote of his experiences while he was a student at Kotzebue High School and was attending college classes as well as playing on the school's basketball team. He graduated in May 1995. He took a year off after high school and before starting at Fort Lewis College in Durango, Colorado, to work as a stocker at one of the main groceries in Kotzebue, Alaska Commercial Company, generally referred as A. C. He also performed general maintenance duties for the local Native regional corporation, NANA. He plans to major in accounting.

Julia Jones Stalker, "Early Lessons Learned from Grandparents," "Eskimo Dance: A Tradition of My People" and "Native Food Nourishes the Body and More." Iñupiaq Julia Jones Stalker, Iñupiaq name Anausuk, was born on July 10, 1962, in Selawik, Alaska, a village southeast of Kotzebue on the Selawik River. She has used her Iñupiaq/English skills to work in bilingual/bicultural educational programs with Ruthie Sampson, another contributor. While a student writer, Julia became interested in a new subsistence activity for her, whale hunting. She has since moved to the village of Point Hope on the northwestern coast of Alaska, where whale hunts take place annually in the spring. She grew up in a family of six children—hunting, fishing, and camping. Julia is a mother of four.

Mark Tucker, "Halloween Mask." Yup'ik Mark Tucker was born February 19, 1963, in Emmonak, a coastal village in southwestern Alaska by the delta of the Yukon River. He wrote this story while working as a teacher's aide in Emmonak, where he grew up learning to hunt and fish as well as to Eskimo dance. His professional plans include becoming a bilingual instructor for the Lower Yukon School District in southwestern Alaska. He grew up in a family of five children with Yup'ik-speaking parents who hunted and fished as part of their traditional life-style. In the summer, he fishes commercially for salmon.

Luci Washington, "Dancing at a Traditional Potlatch." Yup'ik Luci Washington was born May 3, 1950, in St. Michael, Alaska, a village on the Norton Sound south of Nome. She wrote "Dancing at a Traditional Potlatch" while working as an educational aide in St. Michael and attending college part-time with the goal of becoming a bilingual teacher. She grew up in a family of twelve children, who were raised traditionally on the land. Luci is married to Albert, has three daughters and two adopted sons, and now is a grandmother of nine.

Berda Willson, "Higher Education in Northwest Alaska: A Dream Realized" and "Rescue on the Trail of Ice." Iñupiaq Berda Willson was born May 1, 1940, in Nome, but her family moved to the village of Nuuk when she two months old. She wrote both selections in a magazine article writing class while pursuing a degree in rural development from the University of Alaska. A graduate of Nome Beltz High School in 1958 and of the University of Alaska Fairbanks in 1996, Berda has accomplished her educational goals while raising a family and continuing Iñupiaq traditions. She and her daughter, Melissa, graduated at the same time from the University of Alaska Fairbanks branch campus in Nome.

About the Editors

Susan B. Andrews is an associate professor of humanities at the Kotzebue-based Chukchi Campus, College of Rural Alaska, a division of the University of Alaska. A graduate of Smith College, she also has studied in Paris and completed an advanced degree in journalism at the University of Oregon.

A former television and news director and anchor for KTVF-TV in Fairbanks, she also has produced television documentaries for the Alaska Department of Education including *Our Land, Our Future: The 1991 Amendments to the Alaska Natives Claims Settlement Act* and *Portraits of Leadership: Chief Katlain and Howard Rock*. Her other publications include *New Paths, Old Ways: An Alaska Native Studies Catalog for Teachers* as well as children's stories and general fiction.

With her husband, John Creed, she has four children—Myles, Tiffany, and twins Deirdre and Trevor.

John Creed also is an associate professor of humanities at Chukchi Campus. A graduate of the University of Massachusetts, Amherst, he also studied in Norway and at Ireland's University College Dublin and completed his graduate work at the University of Oregon as well as a secondary teaching certificate from the University of Montana.

He is a former staff writer for the *Fairbanks Daily News-Miner* and former editor of the *Tusraagyugaat*, a bilingual (English/Iñupiaq) newspaper based in Kotzebue. Creed has taught secondary school in Massachusetts and in Noatak, an Iñupiaq village north of Kotzebue. His reporting, feature writing, and columns have appeared in print media in Alaska and nationwide.

Andrews's and Creed's creative work in journalism has won regional and national media honors, including a Silver Gavel Award from the American Bar Association, The Alaska Press Club's Public Service Award, and the Robert F. Kennedy Journalism Award for Outstanding Coverage of the Problems of the Disadvantaged.

About Chukchi News
and Information Service

This volume of Alaska Native writings is the result of a decade of collecting the best writings from a college-level publishing project called Chukchi News and Information Service.

Chukchi News and Information Service is a cultural journalism project originating in Kotzebue, Alaska. The service primarily publishes Eskimo, Indian, and Aleut writings in newspapers and magazines throughout the state of Alaska. Since the writing project's founding in 1988, hundreds of rural University of Alaska students have published their writings in the Alaska press, including the *Anchorage Daily News*, *Tundra Times*, *Tundra Drums*, *Arctic Sounder*, *Nome Nugget*, and the *Fairbanks Daily News-Miner*. As a result, thousands more Alaskans, particularly urban Alaskans, have been offered the insights of "average" citizens in rural Alaska through the mainstream press.

In the late 1980s, journalists John Creed and Susan Andrews had accepted faculty positions at a rural campus of the University of Alaska's statewide system of higher education. A voice from rural Alaska writers seemed largely missing from the mainstream press while student writers demonstrated early on a great potential to speak to an audience far beyond the course instructor and fellow students. The pair worked with just a couple students at first, "test marketing" a few polished class essays that spoke to issues of the day: high airfares in rural Alaska, a danger that some village health aides might lose their jobs, the struggle Natives face within their rapidly changing culture, and other rural issues.

They sent these writings, all about the length of a typical newspaper column, around the state to newspaper editors—who published them!

Soon, as the official conduit for Chukchi students to present their work before the reading public in Alaska, Chukchi News and Information Service was born. Finally, "ordinary" rural and Native people were writing about their own lives, their own issues, their own problems, and their own solutions, from a rural Alaska point of view.

As the decade of the 1990s turned, Chukchi News and Information Service, while catching notice both in Alaska and nationally, was becoming a regular fixture in the Alaska press

By 1991, Chukchi News and Information Service had captured some of the most prestigious awards in America's journalism industry, including the Robert F. Kennedy Journalism Award. The RFK Memorial in Washington DC has four programs that honor the work of authors, journalists, and human rights activists who expose the plight of the disadvantaged and fight government oppression: the RFK Book Awards, the RFK Journalism Awards, the RFK Human Rights Award, and the RFK Center for Human Rights.

The judges in the RFK Journalism Awards recognized Chukchi News and Information Service for broadening the range of participants in America's mainstream press with a voice often ignored or unheard, this one from the remote reaches of rural Alaska.

"Once more the diversity of the American press is expanded against the ongoing pressures of conformity," wrote editor Reese Cleghorn in the *Washington Journalism Review* (now *American Journalism Review*), dedicating the well-known trade magazine's lead editorial in June 1991 to Chukchi News and Information Service and its recent First Place honors for students in the annual Robert F. Kennedy journalism awards.

"Students are falling in love with writing and reporting while they struggle to raise families, survive awesome conditions, and bridge two worlds," said Cleghorn, a judge in the RFK Journalism Awards, which included a ceremony in MacLean, Virginia, at the home of the late Robert Kennedy's widow, Ethel Kennedy.

"I found this work truly inspiring," said Cleghorn. "It is a remarkable kind of journalism that triumphs against the odds and enriches the free press with diverse voices, vivid portrayals of Alaska life and bold advocacy on important issues."

Chukchi News and Information Service also captured top honors in other national journalism contests, including the Clarion Award from Women in Communications, Inc., and a Certificate of Recognition from the National Council of Christians and Jews, awards garnered in competition against professional journalists nationwide.

In Alaska itself, Chukchi News and Information Service has won the highest honor in journalism in the state—the Public Service Award from The Alaska Press Club.

The student winners included, from Kotzebue: Hannah Paniyavluk Loon, Blanche Jones Criss, Beatrice Mills, Martha Ramoth, Martha Lee, Lorraine Russell, Benjamin Brantley, Sonny Harris, Janice Salesky, and Kitty Fan Sokkappa. Other students from the Northwest Arctic included Genevieve Norris of Shungnak, James R. Gooden of Kiana, Verné Seum of Kiana, Steve Werle of Noatak, and Grace (Stalker) Kirk of Noatak.

From other regions of rural Alaska: Martha B. Malavansky of St. George, Pribilof Islands; Judy Madros of Nulato; Chris Jacko and Vernajean Kolyaha of Pedro Bay; Flora Johnson and Shirley Ludvick of Illiamna; Steven Angasan of Naknek; Linda Akeya of Savoonga, St. Lawrence Island; Rose M. Heyano of Dillingham; Rena (Boolowon) Booshu of Gambell, St. Lawrence Island; Eleanor Rose Moore of Manokotak; Theresa Prince of Kotlik; Evelyn Wrase of Fairbanks and McGrath; Luci Washington of St. Michael; Connie Irrigoo of Nome; Arlene Barr of Shishmaref; Wilfred "Boyuck" Ryan of Unalakleet; and Mark Tucker of Emmonak.

Index

In the AMERICAN INDIAN LIVES series

*I Stand in the Center of the Good: Interviews with
Contemporary Native American Artists*
Edited by Lawrence Abbott

Authentic Alaska: Voices of Its Native Writers
Edited by Susan B. Andrews and John Creed

*Chief: The Life History of Eugene Delorme,
Imprisoned Santee Sioux*
Edited by Inéz Cardozo-Freeman

Winged Words: American Indian Writers Speak
Edited by Laura Coltelli

Life, Letters and Speeches
By George Copway (Kahgegagahbowh)
Edited by A. LaVonne Brown Ruoff and
Donald B. Smith

*Life Lived Like a Story: Life Stories of Three Yukon
Native Elders*
By Julie Cruikshank in collaboration with
Angela Sidney, Kitty Smith, and Annie Ned

Song of Rita Joe: Autobiography of a Mi'kmaq Poet
By Rita Joe

Catch Colt
By Sidner J. Larson

Alex Posey: Creek Poet, Journalist, and Humorist
By Daniel F. Littlefield Jr.

Mourning Dove: A Salishan Autobiography
Edited by Jay Miller

John Rollin Ridge: His Life and Works
By James W. Parins

*Singing an Indian Song: A Biography of D'Arcy
McNickle*
By Dorothy R. Parker

*Crashing Thunder: The Autobiography of an
American Indian*
Edited by Paul Radin

*Sacred Feathers: The Reverend Peter Jones
(Kahkewaquonaby) and the Mississauga Indians*
By Donald B. Smith

*I Tell You Now: Autobiographical Essays by Native
American Writers*
Edited by Brian Swann and Arnold Krupat

*Chainbreaker: The Revolutionary War Memoirs of
Governor Blacksnake*
As Told to Benjamin Williams
Edited by Thomas S. Abler

Standing in the Light: A Lakota Way of Seeing
By Severt Young Bear and R. D. Theisz